The CASE STUDY
as Research
Method

PRESSES DE L'UNIVERSITÉ DU QUÉBEC
Le Delta I, 2875, boulevard Laurier, bureau 450
Québec (Québec) G1V 2M2
Telephone: 418-657-4399 • Fax: 418-657-2096
Email: puq@puq.ca • Website: www.puq.ca

Diffusion / Distribution:

CANADA and other countries

PROLOGUE INC.
1650, boulevard Lionel-Bertrand
Boisbriand (Québec) J7H 1N7
Telephone: 450-434-0306 / 1 800 363-2864

SUISSE

SERVIDIS SA
Chemin des Chalets
1279 Chavannes-de-Bogis
Suisse

FRANCE

AFPU-DIFFUSION
SODIS

BELGIQUE

PATRIMOINE SPRL
168, rue du Noyer
1030 Bruxelles
Belgique

AFRIQUE

ACTION PÉDAGOGIQUE
POUR L'ÉDUCATION ET LA FORMATION
Angle des rues Jilali Taj Eddine
et El Ghadfa
Maârif 20100 Casablanca
Maroc

Yves-C. GAGNON

The CASE STUDY
as Research Method

A Practical Handbook

2010

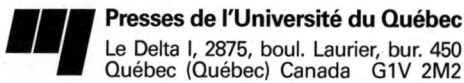

Presses de l'Université du Québec
Le Delta I, 2875, boul. Laurier, bur. 450
Québec (Québec) Canada   G1V 2M2

Bibliothèque et Archives nationales du Québec
and Library and Archives Canada cataloguing in publication

Gagnon, Yves-Chantal

The case study as research method: implementation guide

Translation of: L'étude de cas comme méthode de recherche.

Includes bibliographical references.

ISBN 978-2-7605-2455-2

1. Case method.   2. Social sciences – Research – Methodology.
3. Management – Research – Methodology.   I. Title.

H61.G2413 2010   001.4'33   C2009-942264-6

We are grateful for the financial assistance received from the Government
of Canada under the Book Publishing Industry Development Program (BPIDP).

Publication of this book was made possible through the financial support
of Société de développement des entreprises culturelles (SODEC).

Layout: INFOSCAN COLLETTE-QUÉBEC

Cover: RICHARD HODGSON

Legal deposit – 1st quarter 2010
Bibliothèque et Archives nationales du Québec / Bibliothèque et Archives Canada
Printed in Canada

TABLE OF CONTENTS

FOREWORD

I have been using the case study for almost twenty years as the main research method for all my funded projects, for the case method can provide a sound basis for research. Case studies used as a research tool should be distinguished from another type of case study that is common in teaching, where they are used in a more limited way to illustrate a point or highlight a key learning component (Kennedy 1979; Stake 1994).

Interestingly enough, it used to be much harder to disseminate the results of case-study-based research within the academic community. Quantitative research was the dominant paradigm and the validity of any findings generated by the case method was questioned.

Research based on the case method was viewed with scepticism because of what critics saw as poor design and unsystematic procedures (Yin 1981b; Scholz 2001). This is not surprising since the advocates of positivism focused on the development of universal laws, whereas the case approach focuses on the specific characteristics of the phenomena of interest (Altheide and Johnson 1994). At the time, a number of researchers in the social field argued that the case study was less important than studies producing generalizations for a whole population or for many cases (Stake 1994).

Today, however, the research community has moved almost to the opposite end of the spectrum: not only has the case method become "scientifically correct" but there also seems to be a bias in favour of it within the academic community. In addition, many research programs that base their activities primarily on the quantitative approach often use case studies as a complementary method. This is true for most research fields (at least in the social sciences), for a variety of subjects requiring exploratory research at some level, and in many study contexts. This change is, of course, due in part to the advent of postmodernism, which has affected all disciplines and given new impetus and credibility to the social sciences, arts and philosophy (Agger 1990; Lehman 1991; Lyotard 1979; Richardson 1994). After all, postmodernism is quintessentially a means of challenging any method, theory or discourse that claims sole ownership of the truth or authoritative knowledge (Richardson 1994).

That being said, postmodernism does not automatically reject conventional methods of knowledge acquisition. What it does do is raise questions about such methods and propose other methods that must, in their turn, be assessed as well. Thus while I have defended the qualitative approach to research, I also believe it must meet the same requirements as the quantitative approach. Of course, the qualitative approach is based on a different rationale and different tools, but the validity and reliability of the evidence underpinning the accuracy of the research results must be demonstrated just as clearly and convincingly.

The growing popularity of the case study method has spawned many publications on the subject, but they suffer from two main weaknesses. First, few of them give a full and practical explanation of how to ensure valid, reliable results. Second, hardly any of them provide a structured, integrated and complete guide to conducting a case study. Yin (2008) has perhaps come closest to doing so. The bottom line is that a guide must be a means not only of ensuring *a priori* but also of verifying *a posteriori* the rigorousness of the research process and providing assurance that the findings are accurate.

The purpose of this handbook is, precisely, to give researchers a tool to help them make an informed decision on whether the case method is appropriate and, if it is, to provide them with a guide to help them conduct the study with the required degree of rigour. The handbook covers the appropriateness and usefulness of the case study method, ways of ensuring accuracy of results, the required preparatory work, case selection, data collection, data analysis, and dissemination of results. The objective of each of the above stages is outlined, along with the main steps to be carried out.

As one would expect, this handbook is full of practical examples with a focus on the various components of the research process rather than on the results. One particular example is used throughout the guide so that the reader can follow a specific case study from start to finish. It involves a research project that I carried out on the behaviour exhibited by executives of medium-sized businesses during the introduction of new technologies. I chose it because it formed the basis of my Ph.D. thesis and the work was closely and continuously supervised by a committee of three professors, one of whom was inclined towards the quantitative approach in his thinking and research activities. The principles and philosophy underpinning the quantitative approach were therefore a constant in my thesis project. The thesis itself is over 300 pages long and describes in detail every stage in the case study, the rationale behind it, the steps in it and the results achieved. An entire chapter is devoted to showing how, in practical terms, the reliability and validity of the data has been ensured. The results have been published in articles in two international journals (Gagnon and Toulouse 1993, 1996), which is to say the approach has been subject to further peer review and found to be sound.

After completing my thesis, I decided to generalize my research results by applying a quantitative approach and, in particular, developing and administering a questionnaire. Once again, the results were reported in two scholarly publications (Gagnon 2001; Gagnon, Sicotte and Posada 2000).

Many other examples are given to illustrate specific aspects of the case method. They show that the method is applicable to a broad range of fields in addition to management, the discipline from which my core example is taken. To make this handbook as useful as possible as a practical guide, I also provide a step-by-step checklist in an appendix.

Of course, in preparing a practical guide, one has to make choices. I wanted to include only points that would help researchers carry out case studies, while ensuring that the approach was rigorous. Accordingly, this handbook does not include a more philosophical, or epistemological, section outlining the various schools of thought on, and possible approaches to, planning and executing each stage and step. Nor does it revisit the main debates and arguments on the case study as a research method or take a position on them. The reader should therefore use and judge this handbook with these considerations in mind.

INTRODUCTION

uman and social systems are complex. Understanding phenomena related to such systems demands a holistic approach, which can produce not only detailed descriptions of situations and events but also an in-depth understanding of the actors involved, their feelings and the interactions among them.

Only qualitative research methods can provide a comprehensive view of this type (Benbasat, Goldstein and Mead 1983; Eisenhardt 1989; Patton 1982; Worthman and Roberts 1982). A case study, in particular, makes it possible to observe and analyze phenomena as a single, integrated whole (Bullock 1986). Quantitative methods, though useful, cannot do so, for their main tool, the questionnaire, is based on respondents' considered answers, and as we know 95% of human thoughts are unconscious (Fauconnier 1997; Schank 1998; Wegner 2002; Woodside and Wilson 2003; Zaltman 2003) and individuals have limited awareness of their own thought processes (Van Someren, Barnard and Sandberg 1994; Witte 1972; Woodside and Wilson 2000).

Before going further, we should clarify what we mean by method. We will use Aktouf's (1987: 20) definition of method as "the logical procedure employed by a science, i.e. the set of specific practices it uses to render the development of its demonstrations and theories clear, understandable and irrefutable."

As the case method provides an in-depth understanding of phenomena, their constitutive processes and the actors involved, some scholars believe it is best suited to theory building (Dyer and Wilkins 1991; Eisenhardt 1989; Gersick 1988; Harris and Sutton 1986; Woodside and Wilson 2003). But others, including some proponents of grounded theory, argue that it is equally appropriate for validating a theory (Anderson 1983; Eisenhardt 1989; Glaser and Strauss 1967; Pinfield 1986; Richards and Richards 1994; Strauss and Corbin 1990). Finally, some maintain that it is possible to develop a research design that combines theory building and verification. On this view, a case study can serve to generate a new theory, which can then be tested immediately using measurable constructs and falsifiable hypotheses (Eisenhardt 1989; Gladwin 1989; Howard and Morgenroth 1968; Woodside and Wilson 2003).

More precisely, the case method is said to be appropriate for describing, explaining, predicting or controlling processes associated with a variety of phenomena at the individual, group and organizational levels (Woodside and Wilson 2003). The combination of these four functions is also possible. Describing means answering the questions who, what, when, how (Eisenhardt 1989; Kidder 1982); explaining means attempting to answer the question why; predicting means producing short-term and long-term forecasts of future psychological states, behaviours or events; and controlling means trying to influence cognition, attitudes and behaviours in an individual case (Hersen and Barlow 1976; Woodside and Wilson 2003).

The main advantages of case research are that it can produce an in-depth analysis of phenomena in context, support the development of historical perspectives and guarantee high internal validity,

which is to say that the observed phenomena are authentic representations of reality. In short, the case study is adaptable to both the
context and the researcher.[1]

But when using the case method for research purposes, we
must always bear in mind that it also suffers from weaknesses. First,
it is time-consuming for both the researcher and the subjects. Secondly, the external validity of the results is problematic, for it is difficult for another researcher to reproduce a case study. Finally, the
case method has significant shortcomings when it comes to the generalizability of the results. There is little chance that comparable studies will be conducted to generalize the theory inferred from the case
study or to make the results applicable to an entire population (Lecompte
and Goetz 1982; Lucas 1974; McMillan and Schumacher 1984; Whyte
1963; Worthman and Roberts 1982). This is unsurprising, for the specificity, diversity and narrow focus of a case study are not readily compatible with attempts to achieve a universal scope. For one thing, the
pursuit of generalizability can distract the researcher from specific
features of the case at hand that could be important for a full understanding (Stake 1994). For another, excessive use of empirical data
with a view to generalization will lead almost inevitably to an overly
complex theory in which it is difficult to distinguish between general
relationships and those that are particular to the specific case.

It must therefore be accepted that the result of a case study
is, more often than not, an idiosyncratic theory, which is to say that
it applies to a particular phenomenon or a specific process (Eisenhardt
1989). For example, in their research on changes in life courses in
western Nepal and eastern India over the previous 20 years, Bagchi
et al. (1998) studied the experiences of the inhabitants of 17 villages
and concluded that it was unclear to what extent the evidence from
one community was generalizable to the other villages. However, a
case study can help refine a theory by adding details or it can establish the limits of a generalization. As Stake (1994) notes, we have lost
confidence in the general law that holds that children of separated
parents are better off in their mother's custody since a single case of
a child mistreated by his mother was documented.

This last weakness, the difficulty of generalization, can
however be overcome by complementing the case study with quantitative research (Stake 1994; Scholz 2001; Woodside and Wilson 2003).

---

1.   The singular is generally used in this handbook but it applies equally to research
       teams.

For example, the results of the case study can be used to develop quantitative data collection methods to be applied to a statistically representative sample of the population, as I did in my study of business executives and new technologies. The results of the case studies were used to develop a questionnaire which, after pretesting, was administered to a statistically representative sample of the population of executives of medium-sized businesses engaged in the process of introducing new technologies. This approach made it possible to construct a well-grounded questionnaire based on conditions at medium-sized businesses.

The important point here is that case research must be governed by scientific standards and case studies must be conducted with at least as much rigour as studies that use quantitative research methods (Yin 2003). A case study must be founded on systematic procedures through which the validity and reliability of the evidence and the results can be demonstrated. As Eisenhardt (1989) observes, this depends in large part on the researcher's rigour in carrying out each step in the research process.

Hence the importance of following a practical guide such as this one. We will describe the stages in the process and each step in detail. While the steps will be presented in sequential order, they must often be conducted iteratively (Eisenhardt 1989). Each chapter of this handbook covers one of the stages, explaining and detailing the content of Table 1 below. The next chapter therefore deals with the first stage: assessing the appropriateness of using the case method.

Table 1
Case Study Handbook

STAGE 1 – ASSESSING APPROPRIATENESS AND USEFULNESS

Objective: *Determine whether the case method is relevant and appropriate.*

STEP	OBJECTIVE
1. Define your approach.	Consider whether your perspective is constructivist.
2. Outline the research problem.	Determine whether theoretical foundations already exist.
3. Determine whether the problem is of the exploratory or raw empirical type.	Make sure the problem lends itself to the case method.
4. Answer preset questions to determine the appropriateness of conducting a case study.	Check whether problem characteristics are compatible with the case method.

STAGE 2 – ENSURING ACCURACY OF RESULTS

Objective: *Show that results are rigorous and representative and that they correspond to reality.*

Internal Reliability

OBJECTIVE: *Show that other researchers would arrive at essentially the same conclusions if they analyzed and interpreted the same evidence.*

STEP	OBJECTIVE
1. Use concrete and precise descriptors.	Make as few inferences as possible.
2. Safeguard the raw data.	Make it possible to check the accuracy of the interpretations.
3. Involve several researchers in the study.	Avoid errors of perception or interpretation (bias) on the part of the researcher.
4. Confirm the collected data.	Make sure the data is consistent with the observed reality.
5. Have the interpretation of the data reviewed by peers.	Make sure other researchers interpret the data in a similar way.

External Reliability

OBJECTIVE: *Show that another independent researcher looking at the same cases or similar cases would arrive at essentially the same results.*

STEP	OBJECTIVE
6. Establish the researcher's position.	Describe the various facets of the observed reality and state the point of view from which the observations were made.

STEP	OBJECTIVE
7. Describe the informant selection process and demonstrate its soundness.	Specify the groups and sources from which the data was obtained.
8. Describe the relevant physical, social and interpersonal characteristics of each research setting.	Make it easier to understand the data analysis and to replicate the study.
9. Clearly define the study's concepts, constructs and units of analysis.	Enable other researchers who want to conduct a comparable study to work from similar foundations.
10. Describe the data collection strategy.	Make it possible for other researchers to use the research report as a manual to replicate the data collection process.

Internal Validity

OBJECTIVE: *Make sure the description of the phenomenon is an accurate representation of the observed reality.*

STEP	OBJECTIVE
11. Control for the effects of the observer's presence.	Avoid ethnocentrism and perceptual bias.
12. Select a representative sample.	Prevent distortions due to sampling.
13. Develop and maintain a chain of meaning and a data definition table for each case.	Neutralize the effects of mid-study changes.
14. Identify and exclude alternative explanations.	Support the validity of the conclusions.

External Validity

OBJECTIVE: *Produce results that can be compared and contrasted with other cases.*

STEP	OBJECTIVE
15. Control for the effects of study site specificities.	Avoid idiosyncratic results.
16. Avoid over-studied sites.	Improve the representativeness of the results.
17. Choose cases that are replicable over time and maintain an up-to-date history of each.	Avoid history effects.

Construct Validity

OBJECTIVE: *Show that the abstract terms and meanings are applicable over time and across sites and populations.*

STEP	OBJECTIVE
18. Select cases with characteristics that meet the initial research objectives.	Observe phenomena relevant to the constructs of interest.

19. Choose or develop appropriate measures for purposes of data collection, analysis and interpretation.	Make sure the indicators accurately measure the constructs.
20. Use as many information sources as possible and use triangulation.	Minimize the observer's effect on the phenomenon of interest.
21. Explain the research protocol and present the data honestly.	Report the results in a transparent manner.

STAGE 3 – PREPARATION

Objective: *Have a sufficiently elaborate and precise research framework to ensure rigorous data collection.*

STEP	OBJECTIVE
1. Frame the research question.	Write a clear research question that reflects the researcher's starting point.
2. Choose between a single- or multiple-case study.	Determine the appropriate approach for the research question.
3. Determine the main data collection technique and potential data sources.	Lay the foundations of the data collection strategy.
4. Identify the target population and establish case selection criteria.	Choose a research setting appropriate to the research question.
5. Develop data coding instruments, protocols and schemes.	Determine what data to focus on during data collection and establish rules for data analysis.
6. Become familiar with the phenomenon of interest.	Hone and enrich the materials produced in the previous steps.

STAGE 4 – SELECTING CASES

Objective: *Find enough cases that meet the criteria and make sure the study can be conducted within budget and on schedule.*

STEP	OBJECTIVE
1. Acquire thorough knowledge of the workings of the environment under study.	Lay the groundwork for identifying potential cases and contacting subjects to obtain their active participation.
2. Make sure you have no other professional relationship with the subjects.	Ensure impartiality towards each case.
3. Consider the geographic distribution of cases.	Make sure the study can be conducted within budget and on schedule.
4. Recruit at least one more than the necessary number of cases to ensure rigour.	Guard against the possibility of case mortality.

STAGE 5 – COLLECTING DATA

Objective: *Gather rich, credible raw data, while observing rules of ethics.*

STEP	OBJECTIVE
1. Gain acceptance in the research setting.	Establish a relationship of trust with the subjects.
2. Be observant and practice active listening.	Gather as much significant information as possible.
3. Use as many information sources as possible.	Make it possible to calculate measures of agreement and bolster the validity of the data.
4. Fine-tune the data collection strategy and adapt it to each case.	Make sure you can gather reliable and valid data, while treating your subjects with respect.
5. Develop and maintain a data definition table and a chain of evidence for the collected data.	Maintain consistency in the meanings ascribed to the data and enable an outsider to track the evidence.
6. Manage the collected data on each case in a structured and orderly manner.	Build a reliable, solid database to support valid data analysis and interpretation.
7. Make a smooth exit from the research sites.	Avoid disrupting the research setting.

STAGE 6 – ANALYZING DATA

Objective: *Perform a systematic and fruitful analysis of the collected data.*

STEP	OBJECTIVE
1. Purge the collected data.	Make sure the data is relevant, in an appropriate format, and that the source and data collection method are known.
2. Code the collected data on each case.	Organize and sort the data to facilitate analysis.
3. Analyze the coded data.	Make the data speak by uncovering patterns.
4. Write a description of each case.	Organize the information that supports the patterns found in the analysis into a narrative.

STAGE 7 – INTERPRETING DATA

Objective: *Produce tested, plausible theoretical explanations of the phenomenon of interest.*

STEP	OBJECTIVE
1. Generate proposed explanations of the phenomenon based on the results of the data analysis.	Develop a theoretical explanation for each case in its local context.
2. Check the proposed explanations against the data.	Make sure the ideas are fully and concretely supported by the data on each case.
3. Compare the proposed explanations that pass the evidence test with the existing literature.	Use any divergences as a springboard for further reflection about the proposed explanations in order to support the theory-building process.

STAGE 8 – REPORTING RESULTS

Objective: *Make a contribution to the body of knowledge on the phenomenon and share it with the scientific and professional communities.*

STEP	OBJECTIVE
1. Decide on the type of report.	Determine the appropriate form for the content.
2. Determine the requirements of the vehicle and characteristics of the target audience.	Suit the format and content of the message and the register of the language to the vehicle.
3. Prepare an outline.	Determine the main points of the message and the structure through which it will be conveyed.
4. Write the scientific article or paper, focusing on clarity, concision and the use of appropriate language.	Present the content in a cogent and credible manner to make it more likely the article or paper will be accepted.

STAGE 1

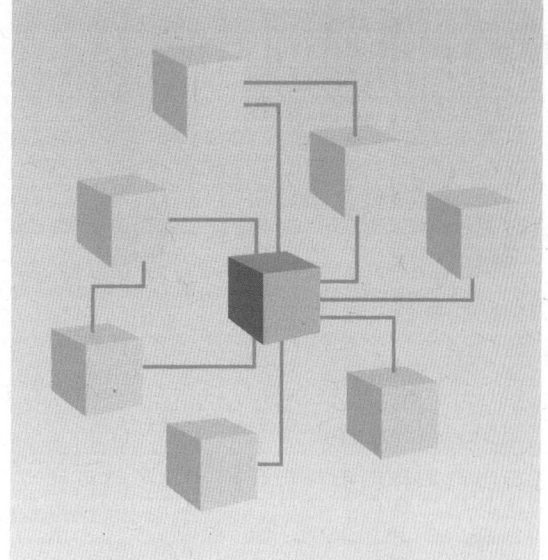

ASSESSING
APPROPRIATENESS
AND USEFULNESS

T he purpose of the first stage in conducting a case study is to determine whether the case method is appropriate to the subject at hand. To do so, the researcher should begin by considering his underlying approach, which is to say his intellectual framework, way of thinking and philosophical underpinnings (Aktouf 1987).

STEP 1.1 Define your approach

A researcher who is considering conducting a case study, or using any other qualitative research method, should subscribe to the constructivist approach, which holds that society is not a given, as it is for the positivists, but rather constructed through the relationships individuals forge with each other (Hagedorn 1983). Investigators who adopt this standpoint strive to understand the behaviour of individuals by examining the influence of their environment on their actions (McMillan and Schumacher 1984). They therefore attempt to probe deeper than the information yielded by quantitative research methods, which are useful but focus on testing selected variables without fully taking into account the context in which they are being measured (Yin 1981a). The qualitative researcher wants not only to determine the correlations among the variables but also to know how and why those correlations exist (Eisenhardt 1989; Mintzberg 1979). It can therefore be said that deciding to carry out a case study is not just a methodological choice but also affects what will be studied (Bardin 1996).

From the constructivist point of view, organizations (including businesses) are complex social systems. To understand them, we need detailed descriptions of situations, events, people, interactions and behaviours. We must understand how things happen before considering why. Only qualitative methods can produce information of this type (Patton 1982; Worthman and Roberts 1982). The result "is not a laboratory study of individuals nor even a field study comparing work groups, but rather a case study in which the organization is viewed as an intact, integrated whole" (Bullock 1986: 33).

Clearly, in this case we will adopt an ideographic rather than a nomothetic research strategy. Ideographic research attempts to understand a phenomenon in context, while nomothetic research uses the procedures of the "exact" sciences to arrive at general laws (Franz and Robey 1984; Weick 1984). In ideographic research, the study is designed to increase our understanding of a particular phenomenon rather than to produce generalizable results (Bardin 1996).

For example, when I was researching the technology adoption practices of medium-sized business executives, I approached the businesses, their nature, and the events and processes occurring in them as constructed, in line with the constructivist outlook. Therefore, it was not enough to interview the owners or managers to learn about the operation of their business. We had to investigate all the actors, their behaviours, their interactions, and when and in what specific circumstances the behaviours and interactions occur in each business. So, in addition to describing, dissecting and explaining the behaviour of the medium-sized business executive, we needed to collect precise, detailed data on the dynamics of the technology adoption processes. This meant gathering, in context, exhaustive situation descriptions of those processes, the related events, the interactions among the people involved, and their observable behaviour. I also had to find out about these actors' experiences, beliefs and thoughts with respect to the technology adoption process. The constructivist approach does not regard technology as deterministic. If we approach the technology adoption process from this standpoint, we must attend to: 1) the people involved in the process; 2) the context; 3) the site at which the technology is being introduced. In other words, it is not enough to study the technology to determine its impact on a business.

STEP 1.2   Outline the research problem

To determine the appropriateness of the case method, the nature of the problem under study must also be considered. It must be borne in mind that case studies are best suited to practical issues in which the experience of the subjects is central and the context of the experience is decisive (Benbasat 1984; Benbasat et al. 1987; Bonoma 1983; Roethlisberger 1977). According to Yin (1981a: 98), "The need to use case studies arises whenever: an empirical inquiry must examine a contemporary phenomenon in its real-life context, especially when the boundaries between phenomenon and context are not clearly evident."

We must therefore define the object of study and consider the existing theoretical base on the subject. This entails identifying the phenomenon we are seeking to understand, its context and the main issue it raises. To do so, the researcher is well advised to consider why he or she took an interest in the topic. At this stage, the researcher should also conduct a preliminary survey of the literature to determine what is already known about the phenomenon. However, the research question will be precisely defined only in the next stage.

 ## Determine whether the problem is of the exploratory or raw empirical type

Once the research problem has been roughly defined, we can determine whether the issues it raises belong to one of the two types that most readily lend themselves to case studies, namely exploratory and raw empirical. Investigators who use the case method seek to systematically infer meaning from the events they observe (McMillan and Schumacher 1984; Rothe 1982) but this does not necessarily mean they have no preliminary ideas and conceptions about the research question. If they do, the research can be considered exploratory in nature; if not, it can be considered raw empirical research, in which the researcher is interested in a subject without having formed any preconceived ideas about it (Benbasat et al. 1987; McMillan and Schumacher 1984; Whyte 1963).

An exploratory study deals with a subject that is clearly important but has been previously neglected for various reasons. Raw empirical research precedes an exploratory study, insofar as the research potential of the subject has not yet been established with sufficient certainty to warrant tackling it in earnest (Benbasat et al. 1987; Gagnon and Landry 1989; McMillan and Schumacher 1984; Whyte 1963).

Answer preset questions to determine appropriateness

Researchers should consider four points before undertaking a case study (based on Benbasat et al. 1987: 372). The research problem is compatible with the case study method if each of the following questions can be answered in the affirmative:

1. Can the phenomenon of interest be studied outside its natural setting?

2. Must the study focus on contemporary events?

3. Is control or manipulation of subjects or events unnecessary?

4. Does the phenomenon of interest enjoy an established theoretical base?

In the case of my study of the technology adoption behaviour of medium-sized business executives, the answers to the four questions confirmed that the case study approach was appropriate. Regarding Question 1, the executive's technology adoption behaviour is related to the specific setting where the technology is being introduced: it cannot be properly understood without taking into account corporate culture (which is likely to be quite different at a medium-sized business than a major corporation) and the existing relationships among the people who will be affected, directly or indirectly. Each technology adoption setting is different and the business executive's behaviour may be more entrepreneurial or more administrative, depending on the context. It was therefore important to understand the interaction between the technology and the environment in which it was being introduced.

Regarding Question 2, post hoc examination of the technology adoption process would not have enabled us to identify and understand all the concomitant events. Some events may fade in importance over time; for example, in one case I observed, an air conditioning failure on a sweltering hot day had a devastating effect on the patience and morale of shop-floor employees, who were already under pressure due to problems with the introduction of a new technology. The upshot was a walk-out, sparking second thoughts about the technology. However, six months later, in the dead of winter, only the technical problems were cited to explain the reservations about the project.

Question 3 can also be answered in the affirmative. Not only were control or manipulation of the subjects and events unnecessary, but they would have altered the phenomenon of interest.

Finally, with respect to Question 4, there was indeed a solid theoretical base for research on technology adoption and on the differences between entrepreneurial and administrative behaviour. However, those two bodies of literature had never been used in conjunction to study business executives' technology adoption practices.

Once it has been established that the problem of interest meets the criteria for case research, the next stage is to consider how to proceed in order to obtain accurate results.

STAGE 2

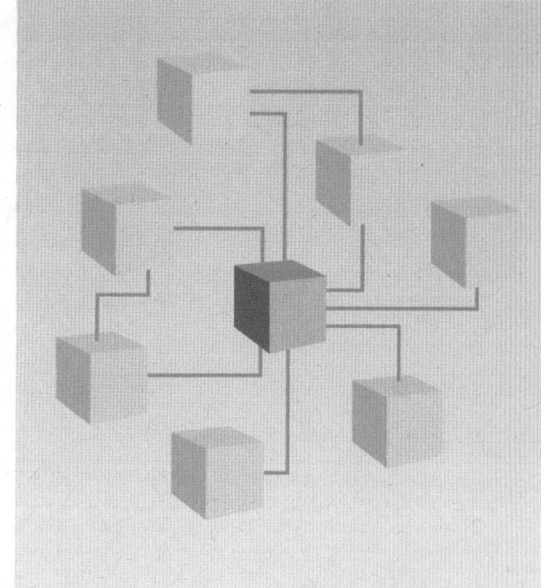

ENSURING
ACCURACY
OF RESULTS

The accuracy of the results must be a paramount concern for the researcher from the beginning to the end of the study. Therefore, the steps that will be taken in the course of the project to ensure accuracy should be considered at the very outset, as soon as the appropriateness of the case method has been established. The purpose of this vital stage, which should inform all the others, is to demonstrate not only that the results were obtained through a rigorous process, but also that they correspond to reality.

The value of a scientific study depends in large part on the investigator's ability to demonstrate the accuracy of the results. This is particularly true for qualitative research methods such as case studies: since these methods are more flexible, they can attract sloppy researchers who hope to avoid the direct evaluation to which the results produced by quantitative and experimental methods are automatically subjected (Hlady Rispal 2002a, b; Kvale 1987).

The concept of accuracy embraces two components: reliability and validity. Reliability relates to the consistency of the observations, meaning the replicability of the results: if the same phenomenon were investigated by other researchers using the same methodology, they should arrive at roughly the same conclusions (Kvale 1987). Validity relates to the connection between the results and reality. A study is valid if the constructs developed by the researcher are good representations or measures of the categories of human experience under observation. Reliability is a necessary condition for validity but does not guarantee it (Bachelor 1992; Light, Singer and Willett 1990).

When we conduct a case study for research purposes, we are examining the interactions among a number of variables in a natural setting, often without any preconceptions. The researcher plays a decisive role at every stage of the process: data collection, analysis and interpretation. Therefore, the researcher's actions and personal characteristics can have a significant direct impact on the accuracy of the results. There are three classic types of bias that investigators are liable to introduce: the holistic illusion, which consists in ascribing greater connectedness and consistency to events than they actually possess (for example, by ignoring facts that do not fit); the elite bias, which consists in attaching greater weight to information from informants who express themselves clearly than to reports from less articulate informants; and over-assimilation, whereby the researcher accepts the facts and perceptions conveyed by local informants whole cloth, surrendering his or her own vision and critical faculties.

Personal characteristics that can introduce bias into the analysis and interpretation of the evidence include individual differences, gender, age, theoretical orientation, the investigator's history with the object of study, and level of experience (Hill, O'Grady and Price 1988; Landry and Farr 1980). Psychological variables such as self-confidence, level of anxiety and cognitive complexity can also come into play (Landry and Farr 1980). The researcher's history and expectations can therefore introduce idiosyncratic elements (Bachelor 1992; Beutler and Hamblin 1986).

To ensure the accuracy of the results, the researcher's first task is therefore to detect potential sources of bias or contamination and address them. To do so, the researcher may have to apply measures that can appear contradictory at first glance. It is illusory to think that we can obtain results that are entirely reliable and valid. For one thing, in qualitative research it is difficult if not impossible to demonstrate reliability and validity in a precise, numerical manner, as one can in quantitative research. For another, techniques for enhancing reliability and validity operate, more often than not, by reducing the impact of the researcher's subjectivity as far as possible, or by providing information to enable others to check the process through which the results were obtained (Guba 1981). This chapter, which is largely based on Lecompte and Goetz (1982), covers the factors that must be borne in mind and the steps to be taken in order to increase reliability and validity.

Reliability can be divided into two components: internal reliability and external reliability. Internal reliability means that other investigators would arrive at essentially the same findings if they were to analyze and interpret the data produced by the study. In other words, the conclusions drawn from the evidence by multiple independent observers and coders would be sufficiently consistent to describe the phenomenon in a similar way and come to the same conclusions about each case. External reliability means that an independent researcher using the same methodology would obtain essentially the same data if he or she were to observe the same environment or a similar environment.

INTERNAL RELIABILITY

To enhance *internal reliability*, it is recommended that the researcher take the following five steps, inasmuch as it is possible to do so.

Use concrete and precise descriptors

Using the most concrete and precise descriptors possible means reporting what people said word for word and describing their behaviours or activities in narrative form. Inferences based on sources other than direct observation should be kept to a minimum. For every inference drawn, one must ask whether it is appropriate and whether all alternative explanations can legitimately be dismissed (Yin 2003).

Safeguard the raw data

The raw data must always be kept accessible so that other researchers can check and confirm the accuracy of the interpretations. Whenever possible, it is preferable to use electronic recording devices: the tape recorder, camcorder and camera should be regarded as standard data collection tools.

Unfortunately, this was impossible to do in my study of business executives, as I was researching a situation in which several actors were intervening simultaneously, and in any event I was prevented from doing so by confidentiality agreements with the informants. However, I did keep copies of written documents or transcribed excerpts when I could. Observations were written down immediately and all the evidence was promptly labelled and entered in a file for each observation site.

STEP 2.3 Involve several researchers in the study

Time and budget permitting, it is always preferable for several researchers to be involved in a study. This is one of the most effective ways to ensure internal reliability. To be sure, a single investigator can perform an excellent analysis, provided he or she controls for potential bias, but having a number of researchers involved can make it much easier to ensure the accuracy of the results. If independent analysts agree among themselves, it can be assumed that the results will not be skewed by their individual characteristics (Andrew 1985; Bachelor 1992; Cone and Foster 1982). This also increases the potential for creativity in the analysis and interpretation of the evidence (Bachelor 1992; Eisenhardt 1989; Miles and Huberman 1994; Taylor and Bogdan 1984).

When there are several researchers working on a project, they evaluate the evidence individually and then compare notes. Areas of disagreement are identified and discussed in order to deepen the analysis and interpretation of the data and confront divergences; the tension of intersubjectivity can help guarantee a measure of objectivity (Halling and Leifer 1991). In this case, we can speak of interjudge agreement, which does not however necessarily guarantee that the results correspond to reality, i.e., that they are valid (Berk 1979; Carmines and Zeller 1979). The evaluators may be very reliable and still be detached from the constructs of interest; in other words, the judges may all err in the same way.

In their study of the politics of strategic decision-making in high-velocity environments, Eisenhardt and Bourgeois (1988) reported that after collecting qualitative and quantitative information, each of them independently analyzed one type of evidence. They developed their own preliminary hypotheses, traded the results of their analyses, and worked to find patterns in the data by consensus.

STEP 2.4 Confirm the collected data

At some point, we need to go back to the key informants to confirm what the observer saw and recorded, in order to make sure that those observations correspond to reality and have not been unduly affected by the investigator's bias. This can be done during the data collection stage or during data analysis and interpretation. The informants' points of view can also be most useful for arbitrating differing perceptions on the part of the researchers.

In my research on the behaviour of business executives, this confirmation process was conducted mainly with the developers. We met frequently to discuss my observations, which sometimes led me to check and clarify other evidence with other sources.

 Have the interpretation of the data reviewed by peers

It is always preferable to have the researcher's interpretation of the evidence reviewed by peers to see whether they arrive at similar conclusions. This is usually done at the reporting stage. It can also be a good idea to ask colleagues to review the research report. The point here is not to expunge the investigator's subjective experience from the report; on the contrary, the document should be informative regarding the researcher's expectations, influences and possible biases. The report should be framed in the most concrete and precise terms possible. One simple way to do so is to directly quote the informants and/or documents from which the information in the report was obtained.

In my study of business executives, I quoted subjects' comments and the documents I had consulted verbatim wherever possible. This technique was used to produce the case descriptions in both the appendix and the summary included in the body of the report. As a doctoral candidate, I was also able to hold frequent discussions throughout the research process with a committee of three experienced researchers with different fields of interest (unfortunately, after completing a Ph.D. thesis, a researcher seldom has the opportunity to benefit from this type of advice in subsequent work), and I discussed my analysis and interpretation of the evidence with fellow doctoral candidates who were doing similar research on companies with comparable characteristics.

EXTERNAL RELIABILITY

External reliability is established by demonstrating that independent researchers would discover the same phenomenon or develop the same constructs if they applied the same methodology in a similar or identical setting. To be sure, this is no easy matter, particularly for a case study, which by its nature is unique and often idiosyncratic. However, external reliability can be significantly enhanced if five major threats are addressed through the steps described below.

STEP 2.6 Establish the researcher's position

Researchers must always establish to what extent they are part of the phenomenon they are studying and define their precise position. They must consider how their position may be influencing their organization of the reality they are observing. The investigator's role and position in the phenomenon he or she is studying must always be stated when publishing the research results, so the reader is aware of the standpoint from which the reported observations were collected.

A case study depends, to some extent, on the type of social relationship the researcher establishes with informants. Some investigators confine themselves to a professional relationship, while others have been known to form friendships with subjects. The latter course can yield privileged or private information but may also affect the researcher's critical sense. The researcher must be aware of this risk and take care to describe the nature and development of his or her relationship with study participants and informants.

In my study of the behaviour of business executives, I noted on several occasions, in the research report and the articles based on the results, that the evidence was collected by non-participant observation, and the relationship with participants and informants was one of trust and not purely professional, though neither was it a prelude to friendship.

STEP 2.7 Describe the informant selection process

External reliability requires a careful choice of informants and a full description of the process by which they were selected. One must be able to provide a list of types informants and their characteristics, for in a case study the quality of the collected information largely depends on the informants from whom it was obtained. The characteristics in question include the relevant personal traits of the researcher, the informants and the other participants in the phenomenon. This description of the study population and the informants must appear in all documents in which the research results are reported. It is imperative that the researcher indicate the groups and sources from which his or her information and observations were drawn.

My report on the study of business executives' behaviour included this type of information. Furthermore, an appendix detailing the standard structure of the files on the 11 observed technology adoption processes provided the full data and the sources (name of informant, title of document consulted, etc.).

STEP 2.8 Describe the characteristics of each research setting

The situations and social conditions in which the data was collected should be described. For example, in his study of education in an ethnic neighbourhood in a major city, Ogbu (1974) showed that the information provided by parents in a school environment was not the same as that provided in a home setting. This can often be the case with the evidence obtained from a study participant: for example, the information may differ depending on whether the participant is being interviewed alone or in a group. Therefore, the specific environment at each study site – i.e. the physical, social and interpersonal context in which the data was collected – must be described as clearly as possible. This enhances our understanding of the interpretation of the data and also provides points of reference for anyone who might wish to replicate the study.

In my study of business executives, I included an appendix to the research report providing a detailed description of the environment at each business and the specific characteristics of each observed technology adoption process. The characteristics of each research site were also summarized in a data coding diagram in another section of the report.

STEP 2.9 Clearly define the study's concepts, constructs and units of analysis

The investigator's premises must be clearly stated, since it is virtually impossible to replicate a study if the concepts, constructs or units of analysis are idiosyncratic, poorly delineated or simply unknown. If we fail to carefully define our categories and their theoretical underpinnings,

there is a risk that our findings will be idiosyncratic or difficult to compare. When the hypotheses and constructs are unclear, the results may also be difficult to understand.

It is therefore vitally important to explicitly state the hypotheses and metatheories underlying the choice of terminology and of data analysis and interpretation techniques. For example, the concept of culture is variously defined by different researchers, schools of thought and disciplines. The constructs used must also be defined in order to enable any other investigator who wants to conduct a similar study to proceed from the same starting point. To be useful, the definitions of the constructs and concepts must be clearly and precisely stated; i.e. we must clarify the specificity of the variable as well as what distinguishes it from other variables, and explain how it can be measured. The definitions should not be the researcher's individual or personal concepts.

This is not to say that researchers cannot develop their own conceptual schema, and choose to dismiss or ignore those used by other investigators. On the contrary: it would be absurd to use a previously established classification only because it is known and easy to apply, if we know that doing so is liable to result in a premature categorization that is ill-suited to the evidence, or in mechanical or reductive standardizations that will render the results trivial. However, researchers who choose to develop their own conceptual scheme must then produce a theoretical analysis of its implicit structure. The analytic units must be clearly defined, which is to say we must know where they begin and end. Finally, the variables on which the data collection and analysis operations were based must be described.

In my study of business executives, the concepts used – technology, technology adoption, company size (small, medium, large), nature and complexity of the technology – were all explicitly defined. The definitions corresponded to those generally used in the literature and therefore were not idiosyncratic.

STEP 2.10 Describe the data collection strategy

Researchers should explain their methods so that others can easily use their publications as a manual to replicate the study, which cannot be done unless the data collection strategy is stated and described in detail.

External reliability is demonstrated by various elements of research publications. The investigator must always provide a description of the study population and of the instruments used for data collection, analysis and interpretation. Once again, the purpose is to make it possible for other researchers to replicate the study.

In my study of business executives, one section of the research report was devoted to a precise description of each of the steps I had followed. Among other things, I explained how the evidence was collected and then analyzed, and finally the process by which it was interpreted.

Table 2 below summarizes the actions that should be taken to establish reliability, and specifies the stage and step to which each action belongs.

Table 2
Ensuring Reliability

Dimension	What it means	What to do	Stage (Step #)
Internal reliability	Data is stable	Use concrete descriptors	Collecting data (3)
		Safeguard raw data	Collecting data (3, 6)
		Use multiple researchers	Analyzing data (3)
		Ask key respondents to confirm observations and evidence	Collecting data (2, 5) Analyzing data (3)
		Have the analysis reviewed by peers	Analyzing data (3) Reporting data (4)
External reliability	Results are replicable	Establish the researcher's position	Preparation (3) Collecting data (3, 4) Analyzing data (3, 4) Reporting data (4)
		Select informants judiciously	Collecting data (4)
		Describe data collection situations and social conditions	Collecting data (3, 6) Analyzing data (4)
		Clearly define the study's premises	Preparation (1)
		Describe the data collection strategy	Reporting data (3, 4)

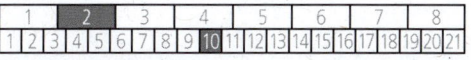

We shall now turn to **validity**. Validity is established by producing a reasonably well-documented and consistent interpretation of the evidence so that other researchers can reach a general consensus (Kvale 1987). Validity also has two sides: internal and external. Internal validity means that the investigator has in fact observed and measured the things he or she set out to observe and measure, and that the descriptions and explanations of the phenomenon of interest are true representations of the observed reality. External validity refers to the extent to which the identification and description of the phenomenon under study are legitimate and comparable; in other words, the degree to which the premises and constructs generated, refined and tested in the course of the study are applicable to other cases, i.e., generalizable. Construct validity is therefore part of external validity, since it refers to the consistency and comparability of the constructs.

INTERNAL VALIDITY

Internal validity is probably the main strength of the case study. Observing informants in their natural environment and collecting data over a long period of time makes it possible to continuously analyze and compare the evidence in order to refine the constructs and make sure they correspond to reality. The following four steps can strengthen internal validity.

 **Control for the effects of the observer's presence**

It is entirely possible and indeed probable that the observer's presence will have an impact on the evidence that is collected (Schwartz and Schwartz 1955). What the observer sees and reports depends on his or her position within the environment under study. It is therefore important for observers to guard against their own ethnocentrism and perceptual biases. To do so, the researcher must submit an explicit retrospective analysis of his or her own position as an observer in the research setting and the relationships he or she established with the informants, which should be as neutral as possible. The researcher must collect evidence from several sources so that measures of agreement can be calculated (Benbasat et al. 1983; Denzin 1978; McMillan and Schumacher 1984), and also make sure his or her constructs are supported by and consistent with the evidence. The same applies to the categories used, which must be meaningful for the participants and reflect their experience of reality.

In my study of business executives, my status was clearly stated several times in the research report. I also used several sources, which made it possible to corroborate the data in many cases. To make sure I had correctly understood the meaning and import of informants' comments, I used semantic tests to specify and clarify the meanings of the terms and concepts used by informants. I also used the rephrasing technique as often as possible.

STEP 2.12 Select a representative sample

When there are too many potential participants or informants, or when the social setting under observation is so complex that continuous observation of all the events, activities or sites is not possible, we need to select a sample from which to collect data. In this case, it is important to prevent any distortions in the raw data or in data analysis or interpretation due to sampling. If we are unable to compile a sample that is representative of the sub-groups, factions, events and social settings that fall within the scope of our study, the results may describe only a segment of the phenomenon, participants or circumstances.

It is very important to establish the characteristics and specific features of the informants, participants and social settings, and to collect evidence from each category. The researcher must strive to establish contacts and relationships with the largest and most diverse selection of informants possible, and to observe a wide range of social settings. Even though it is a theoretical sample, the investigator must make sure that it is representative of the population of informants and participants, as well as of the activities, events and sites associated with the phenomenon.

This should be demonstrated in all reports on the study findings in order to make the results comparable with those of other case studies of the same phenomenon and verifiable using other samples of the same population.

In the case of my study of business executives, the sample and its relationship to the target population were meticulously described in the research report. Each relevant variable was described

and the choices made with respect to each variable were explained and supported. Finally, a detailed description of the sample selection process was also provided.

Develop a chain of meaning and a data definition table

The researcher must be able to deal with any changes that occur during the study. Clearly, the addition, departure or death of participants can affect the evidence. The researcher must ensure that the data collection process is unaffected by changes of this type. This is where the chain of meaning and the data definition table become important, enabling the investigator to compare activities and events even if they occurred at different times and with different participants.

A major change occurred in one case in my study of business executives and new technology. My standard notes, written immediately after each data collection, served as a data definition table and to maintain the chain of meaning. Therefore, the departure of one of the informants did not prevent comparison of the data.

Identify and exclude alternative explanations

The researcher must make sure the conclusions of the study are accurate. The basic strategy for testing data interpretation consists in identifying and excluding other possible explanations of the evidence and looking for counter-evidence that could invalidate the conclusions (Kvale 1987; Miles and Huberman 1994, Patton 1980). Excluding rival explanations requires an exhaustive review of the literature; searching for counter-evidence demands an effective, efficient data classification system.

In their study of the politics of strategic decision-making in high-velocity environments, Eisenhardt and Bourgeois (1988) report that, after going back and forth between the evidence and the hypotheses, they took pairs of firms and listed the similarities and differences. They then used the literature to refine their intuitions and test other explanatory schemes.

EXTERNAL VALIDITY

As we have noted, ***external validity***, which relates to the generalizability of the results, is probably the main weakness of the case study. However, this should not discourage us. As Cronbach (1975) noted, "all generalizations 'decay' like radioactive substances, having half-lives, so that after a time every generalization is more history than science." However, we do need to exercise vigilance in order to produce results that can at least be compared and contrasted with other cases. To maintain external validity, we therefore have to consider the factors that threaten the comparability and transferability of the results. Increasing the number of cases studied will automatically help improve the external validity of the results. But below we also discuss four other methods for enhancing external validity.

STEP 2.15 Control for the effects of study site specificities

Cross-case comparison of constructs is not possible if the construct is specific to a particular group or if the researcher has mistakenly chosen a group to which it does not apply. The constructs developed in a given context may not be comparable because they are specific to the particular case(s). It is therefore important to ascertain that the context selected for the study does not have specific features that will automatically make the results idiosyncratic.

STEP 2.16 Avoid over–studied sites

Choosing a site that is saturated with studies can make the results less representative. It may be assumed that frequently studied groups and cultures differ from other groups. The investigator should therefore choose a site that has not been saturated with repeated observation and investigation, regardless of the nature and purpose of the studies. This is particularly true for new, trendy phenomena that draw researchers working in different fields. For example, for a study of dropping out, a school that has introduced a spectacularly successful program to keep kids in school might not be a good choice, since it is likely to have attracted droves of researchers.

 **STEP 2.17 Choose cases that are replicable over time**

While it is unlikely that the phenomenon of interest will subsequently recur in precisely the same way, the researcher should attempt, as far as possible, to choose for the study a setting in which the observed phenomenon could recur in some form. It is also important to track and record the collected data and its meaning at each point in the study. A variety of data collection strategies should be used to make the results comparable on an ongoing basis. The point is to make sure that the phenomenon studied at the beginning of the process is the same as the one observed subsequently.

In my study of medium-sized business executives, a full report was prepared on the collected data after each site visit, regardless of its nature. Extensive documentation was compiled in this manner, making it possible to determine whether changes had occurred.

CONSTRUCT VALIDITY

Construct validity refers to the extent to which abstract terms and meanings are consistent over time, across sites and populations (Cook and Campbell 1979). As we saw with reliability, the comparability of case studies can be reduced or rendered more difficult by idiosyncratic use of analytic constructs or by generating constructs so specific to a particular case that they cannot be used for cross-case comparison.

 **STEP 2.18 Select cases relevant to the research objectives**

It is very important that the cases selected for observation match the constructs we want to study (Yin 2003).

 **STEP 2.19 Choose or develop appropriate measures**

The indicators used in collecting, analyzing and interpreting the evidence must in fact measure the constructs that have been defined for the purposes of the study.

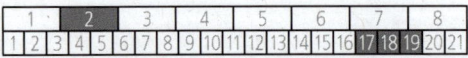

2.20 Use as many information sources as possible

One should always use several information sources and triangulate the data in order to formalize the meanings the participants ascribe to a phenomenon.

2.21 Explain the research protocol and present the data honestly

The evidence should always be presented in a transparent manner and the investigator should demonstrate that the research protocol was followed scrupulously (Yin 2003).

Other steps, which have already been described, also contribute to increasing construct validity. These include keeping a chain of evidence and checking meanings with key informants, making it possible for an outside observer to determine whether the evidence presented accurately reflects the empirical data on which it is based. Having a research team or submitting the study to peer review helps ensure that interpretations of the facts are well grounded and not simply assumed, even when they seem routine or self-evident (Yin 2003).

Table 3 shows the main actions that should be carried out to increase the validity of the data and indicates the stage and step to which the action relates.

Having reviewed all the key points that must be borne in mind in order to ensure that the results of the case study are accurate, the researcher is now ready to proceed to the next steps, beginning with the preparatory work.

Table 3
Ensuring Validity

Dimension	What it means	What to do	Stage (Step #)
Internal validity	Results are credible	Control for effects of observer's presence	Preparation (3, 5) Selecting cases (2) Collecting data (3, 4) Analyzing data (3) Interpreting data (2, 3)
		Select representative samples	Collecting data (4) Reporting data (4)
		Manage effects of change	Selecting cases (4) Collecting data (5)
		Exclude alternative explanations	Analyzing data (3) Interpreting data (3)
External validity and construct validity	Results are transferable	Study several cases	Preparation (2)
		Control for the effects of observation settings	Preparation (4) Selecting cases (1)
		Avoid over-studied sites	Preparation (4) Selecting cases (1)
		Control for history effects	Preparation (4) Collecting data (5) Analyzing data (4)
		Choose cases that are representative of the phenomenon to which the constructs relate	Preparation (4, 6) Selecting cases (1)
		Make sure construct measures are appropriate	Preparation (5) Collecting data (4)
		Present research protocol and data in a transparent manner	Reporting data (3, 4)

STAGE 3

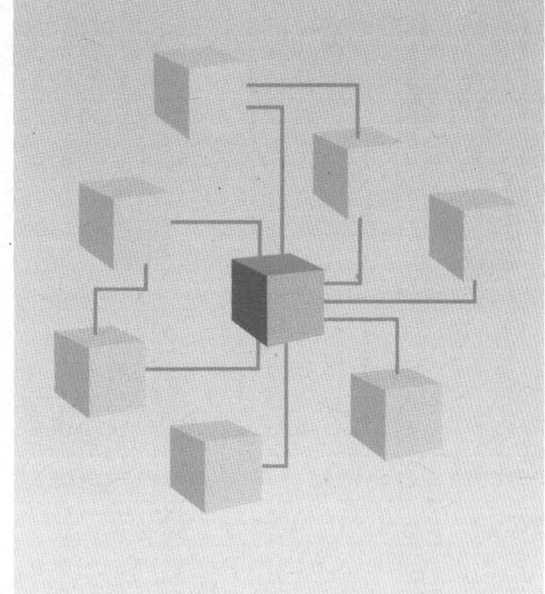

PREPARATION

The preparatory steps discussed in this section should be carried out before undertaking any field work. They are based on my review of the literature and my own practical experience.

Frame the research question

As in most studies, the first thing to do when preparing a case study is to frame a research question, even when working inductively (Bullock 1986; De Weerd-Nederhof 2001; Eisenhardt 1989; Miles and Huberman 1994). The question should be clear and reflect the researcher's starting point (Lucas 1974), based on a thorough review of the literature and, most importantly, the researcher's own thinking about the issue. The investigator must determine not only the phenomenon at the root of the question, which has already been done in the previous stage, but also the aspects of the phenomenon that are of particular interest.

The constructs implied by the question should also be stated (Dyer and Wilkins 1991; Eisenhardt 1989). By construct or concept, we mean a variable that is not concrete or tangible – an intellectual, theoretical construction. The fact that we can measure a construct does not imply that it exists in reality. For example, length is the distance between two points on an imaginary line. A more complex example might be anxiety, leadership, creativity, motivation or satisfaction. The name we apply to the construct is a summary of the definition and usually does not cover its full meaning.

The process of defining the research question is governed by the same logic as the process of testing a hypothesis (Eisenhardt 1989). Before beginning field work, one needs to have at least a crude theoretical framework, while realizing that it may and probably will change in the course of the study (Miles 1979). The pursuit of a theory based on reality, not preconceptions, enters into tension with the need to clarify and focus the study. Research projects that claim to be conducted with no hypotheses usually encounter more difficulties. It is therefore desirable to frame some hypotheses about the research problem, based on the investigator's assumptions, intuitions and suppositions about the phenomenon of interest (Bardin 1996; Dyer and Wilkins 1991; Eisenhardt 1989).

In my study of business executives, I began with a vague curiosity about the fact that technology adoption is so weak in North American businesses. I wondered whether the executive's behaviour could be an important factor in the frequently poor planning of the technology introduction process. As I mulled this, it occurred to me that it might be possible to locate the executive's behaviour on a continuum between entrepreneurial and administrative. My research question therefore became: Where can the executive's behaviour in the new technology adoption process be situated on the entrepreneurial/administrative continuum?

The stated purpose of the life course study by Bagchi et al. (1998) was to determine whether life courses were affected by the political environment. The researchers hypothesized that there would be a considerable impact on life courses where strong and consistent municipal policies were implemented over a long period of time.

In their study of the Cuban missile crisis, Allison and Zelikow (1999) asked the following research question: Why did the Soviet Union decide to place missiles in Cuba? They suggested several starting hypotheses, such as defending Cuba and Cold War politics.

 Choose between a single- or multiple-case study

A single-case study is appropriate primarily to verify a theory, particularly to invalidate the theory or to distinguish it from competing theories, such as the rival explanations of the Cuban missile crisis (Allison and Zelikow 1999; Benbasat, Goldstein and Mead 1983; Whyte 1963; Yin 1981a; Yin 2003). A single-case study can also be used in raw empirical research to investigate a hitherto unexplored phenomenon. But it cannot be assumed that a single-case study is not a useful unit of analysis for theory building, for there are some significant exceptions to this rule. Many studies that have made a contribution to our knowledge of organizations and social systems were based on just one case (Becker et al. 1961; Dyer and Wilkins 1991; Lipset, Trow and Coleman 1956; Selznick 1966) or two (Blau 1955; Crozier 1964). However, a single-case study is even more subject to the problem of generalization that affects the case method as a whole.

For the purposes of psychological research on the effectiveness of a computer-assisted group therapy technique for treating social phobia, Przeworski and Newman (2004) conducted a case study of a subject suffering from social phobia who received six group therapy sessions and carried a pocket computer throughout the treatment. The single-case choice appears warranted here as the researchers were working from a theory on social phobia treatment therapy and their aim was to describe the potential contribution of the computer to the already established therapy.

On the other hand, conducting a multiple-case study makes it possible to draw conclusions from a set of cases. It is usually recommended that four to ten cases be studied (Eisenhardt 1989). Multiple studies are most useful for examining phenomena that are liable to occur in a variety of situations (Romano 1988; Yin 1981a). They can serve to highlight recurring patterns in some variables or to find counter-examples that contradict the defined theoretical constructs (Eisenhardt 1989). The purpose of studying several cases is generally to provide a rich description of the context in which the events occur and to reveal the underlying structure of social behaviour (Light 1979).

It must be borne in mind, however, that the more cases we study, the more arduous the data collection process becomes, from every point of view. Even if we conduct several case studies simultaneously, each will require special attention if we are to properly understand it (Stake 1994). This may lead the investigator to provide less detailed descriptions and to perform a more superficial data collection, leaving aside information on the underlying social dynamics. It is not easy to determine how far the researcher should go in collecting evidence in order to develop a sound theory. But the cases must be limited to the number that can be investigated in sufficient depth, with the available resources, to provide a valid answer to the research question for each case (Dyer and Wilkins 1991).

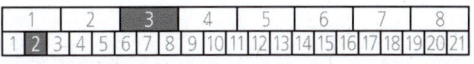

In my study of business executives, I chose to conduct a multiple-case study since the goal was to improve our understanding of the behaviour of medium-sized business executives in the technology adoption process. The review of the literature yielded no established theory on the matter, nor any theory we could validate or invalidate. It was also clear that although our research was confined to medium-sized businesses, the executives were operating in a variety of situations and contexts. A multiple-case study was therefore the most appropriate approach.

In their life course study, Bagchi et al. (1998) set out to compare the impact of different municipal political environments on citizens' lives. It became clear that a multiple-case study was needed to provide a basis for comparison of life courses in different political contexts. The researchers accordingly selected 15 villages in western Nepal and two in eastern Bengal and Bihar for their studies.

In another study, a legal researcher set out to show that adopting a new, three-category definition of acts as voluntary, involuntary or semi-voluntary in criminal law would yield fairer outcomes for defendants. Obviously, at least a few criminal cases had to be studied to test this hypothesis (Denno 2003).

 Determine the main data collection technique and potential data sources

Will you use observation, interviews with the actors to obtain their interpretations of the facts and events, documentary analysis or, better still, a combination of all three techniques?

We must distinguish here between participant and non-participant observation. In non-participant observation, the researcher observes from the outside without becoming directly involved. In participant observation, the researcher shares the lives, activities and feelings of the subjects in the context of the situation he or she wants to analyze (Aktouf 1987). Participant observation has its pitfalls (Becker 1958). In this approach, the researcher is an active agent and may be called upon to play a role that is not consistent with scientific standards. As well, investigators unconsciously become part of the group or organization they are studying, which may affect their objectivity and critical faculties. Finally, researchers may become focused on the participant role, at the expense of the observer role (Yin 2003).

In my research on business executives, I used non-participant observation as the main data collection technique in each of the case studies. The potential sources of information I identified were, in the first instance, the key actors in the technology adoption process, the committees set up for the purpose, and the documentation (suppliers' literature, feasibility studies, profitability studies, implementation plans, project specifications, calls for tenders, bids, contracts, etc.).

Among the key actors, we targeted the developers of the technology in particular, as they were often directly involved in the technology adoption process. There were also the organization's managers, who played an important role in planning and implementing the process once the top-level executive had decided to introduce the new technology. Finally, the executives were among the informants, since they made the decision to adopt the technology. In most of the technology introduction projects we studied, an implementation coordinating group was also set up. This committee generally consisted of developers, experts, managers and sometimes executives. It was important for us to attend these groups' meetings.

In a study of the effect of technological change on pay inequities, Fernandez (2001) opted for a participant observation approach, working on the floor in the two plants where he wanted to conduct case studies. He was hired as a temporary employee in both plants and performed a number of tasks in rotation. This gave him a first-hand, practical view of the impact of technological change on different positions.

 **STEP 3.4**

Identify the target population and establish case selection criteria

This step consists in establishing rules for selecting the cases. The goal is to find appropriate research sites for addressing the research question that has been developed. Obviously, this is a critical step, since the usefulness of the results and what they add to our understanding depend, first and foremost, on choosing a research setting that is relevant to the research question (Patton 1980; Yin 2003). Nothing is more important than suitable case selection (Miles and Huberman 1984; Stake 1994). For this purpose, we first need to identify, on the basis of clearly defined criteria, the target population in which the phenomenon of interest occurs. We must then establish precise rules

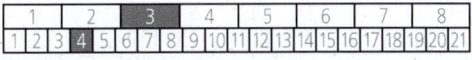

for choosing the cases that will make up the sample (Benbasat et al. 1983; Lucas 1974). These rules often take the form of characteristics that the cases should have.

However, the idea is not to form a statistically representative sample of a population but rather to find the most informative cases. In other words, a case may be more illuminating than it is representative. It is always preferable to learn a good deal from an atypical case than to learn little from an eminently typical case. The primary reason for studying a case is not that it is representative of other cases or illustrates a particular trait or problem but rather that it has specific or shared features that are of interest (Stake 1994). When multiple cases are studied at the same time, they may be different, similar, redundant or varied, but each has a specific character. The researcher attempts to identify both the specific and shared features, and the final result may often be unique for each case.

It is therefore preferable to use theoretical sampling: the cases are not selected for statistical reasons but rather on the basis of representativeness, balance, potential for revealing new information, the research objectives, homogeneousness, or on the contrary maximum variety (Eisenhardt 1989; Eisenhardt and Bourgeois 1988; Gersick 1988; Glaser and Strauss 1967; Harris and Sutton 1986; Hlady Rispal 2002a, b).

A practical example should help clarify the nature of this step. In my study of medium-sized business executives, I realized that the new technology adoption process had specific features in Quebec. I therefore took all Quebec businesses as my target population. To select a sample, I used three main criteria: technology, the size of the business and its line of business. The first involved two dimensions, type and scope. The technology type could be an enterprise information system, a production management system or automation. When it came to scope, I was interested in the full spectrum of projects along a continuum ranging from the introduction of a single technology (i.e. involving only one department of the company) to complex technology (i.e. covering all departments). The larger the number of departments directly affected, the more complex the project was considered to be.

For the second variable, a variety of criteria or a combination of criteria could have been used to classify businesses by size. For the purposes of my study, using a single criterion, number of employees, appeared straightforward and sufficient. Accordingly, we classified manufacturing companies into four categories: small (1 to 49 employees), medium (50 to 249 employees), large (250 to 499 employees) and very large (500 employees and more). For non-manufacturing businesses, the "very large" category was dropped.

The third criterion was line of business (e.g. manufacturing or service).

Crossing the first two variables yielded a grid with nine possible company size/technology type combinations for each point along the complexity of technology continuum, producing the three-dimensional figure shown in Chart 1. This figure was repeated for each line of business, our third variable.

Chart 1
Variables of Study Population

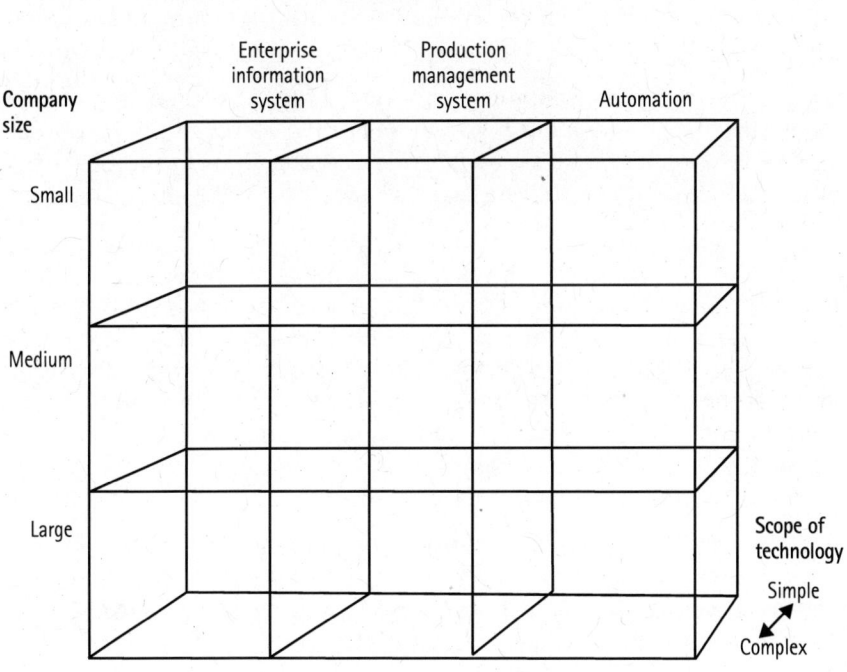

I decided I would need to observe at least three cases for each box in my grid, for a total of 27 cases for each line of business and each level of technological complexity. With the data collection method I was using, direct observation, this did not appear to be physically possible.

I therefore had to confine myself to a limited number of combinations, knowing that this would make it impossible to measure some of the variables.

To classify the companies by type of new technology, I used three categories: enterprise information system, production management system and automation. This decision appeared warranted since I was interested in the adoption of all types of technology. By including different types, I would be able to determine whether business executives followed a similar process regardless of the type of technology being introduced.

When it came to the scope of the technology, I decided to limit the study to the adoption of medium-complexity technology. I therefore examined projects that affected several departments of the company. I decided I had to exclude the extremes (simple and complex) to avoid ending up with conclusions that applied to few cases.

For the company size criterion, I eliminated large and very large businesses, since they have already received considerable attention in studies of technology adoption, while there have been few empirical studies of medium-sized businesses. Moreover, medium-sized companies play a key role in Quebec's economy.

Finally, for line of business, I decided to look at the manufacturing sector, a driver of the Quebec economy and perhaps the sector subject to the strongest pressure to adopt new technologies. It is also the sector in which the consequences of any shortcomings in the technology introduction process are likely to be most dire, and where I had the best chance of finding all three technology types. Of course, this decision prevented me from examining inter-sector differences, but that was not the purpose of my study.

I therefore focused on medium-sized manufacturers that were introducing any of the three technology types at the medium complexity level. Chart 2 below shows the resulting sample. The 11 letters in the squares stand for the cases included in the study.

Chart 2
Variables of Selected Cases

Technology type

Company size	Enterprise information system		Production management system		Automation		Scope of technology
Medium	E	F	B	C	A	D	Fairly complex
	G		H	J	I	K	

 **STEP 3.5** **Develop data coding instruments, protocols and schemes**

The investigator must decide what evidence to focus on and establish rules for analyzing the evidence. For multiple-case studies, this scheme is also used to maintain consistency when comparing data from different sites (Glaser and Strauss 1967; McMillan and Schumacher 1984).

It is also at this stage that the researcher should decide whether to use computer software to analyze the data. If so, he or she must decide what type of computer processing is to be performed and then prepare a list of the software available on the market, find up-to-date information and descriptions of each, watch a demo and, most importantly, read the comments and evaluations in the literature (Richards and Richards 1994). The choice of software should be based on which application best matches the previously identified needs and offers the most features likely to be used by the researcher. Once the choice has been made, the researcher needs to familiarize himself or herself with the application and take training in order to be able to take advantage of all its functions. The use of computer software will be discussed in greater detail in the chapter on data analysis.

For my study of business executives and technology adoption, my survey of the literature turned up an already tested grid which I was able to use to locate the executive's general behaviour along the entrepreneurial/administrative continuum. I was therefore able to use this grid as a frame for coding and analyzing the evidence.

STEP 3.6 Become familiar with the phenomenon of interest

To become familiar with the phenomenon of interest, the investigator may, for example, meet with people who have personal experience with the phenomenon and sound them out, visit sites where the phenomenon has occurred or is occurring, and so forth. This process is useful for adjusting and enriching the materials produced in the previous steps. It also provides the researcher with information on customs and practices in the environment in which the case studies are to be conducted, and on the terminology used by the subjects.

Resources and time permitting, it is advisable to carry out a pilot case study to test the research question, the information gathering tools, the data coding scheme, and so forth. More importantly still, a pilot case study will indicate whether the approach will work with the subjects of the study in real life and whether it is suitable for the purposes of the study. The case should therefore be representative of the subject of the study and allow for easy access to information. The subjects should be enthusiastic about the idea of participating in the study and prepared to accept some experimentation and trial-and-error (Hlady Rispal 2002a, b).

In my study of business executives, I began by meeting with business association representatives who were aware of the issues and with developers and business executives who had been through a technology adoption process. I then observed three cases of technology introduction at different companies, which gave me reason to believe the study had a reasonable chance of success, insofar as my preliminary hypothesis seemed to correspond to reality and my methodology proved functional.

With the research framework established, it is time to go into the field and select cases for observation. This is the subject of the next chapter.

STAGE 4

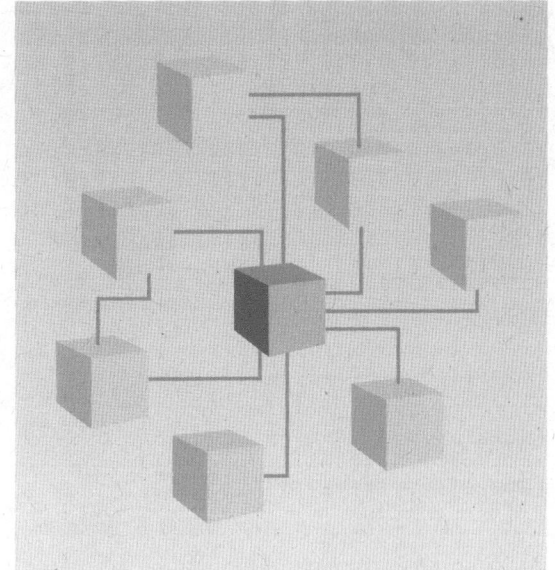

SELECTING CASES

*T*he researcher must devote considerable effort to finding cases that fully meet the criteria that have been established for forming the theoretical sample. And then the selected subjects must be persuaded to participate in the study, which may require some skill. As we have noted, participation in a case study is no trivial matter; it can demand considerable time spread over several sessions and a fairly long period. It also means surrendering privacy by allowing a stranger, the researcher, into the group's inner sanctum. This stage is tricky because the strategies dictated by the study's requirements come up against the constraints created by the specific features of each research setting (Hlady Rispal 2002a, b).

The subjects should be shown that they have an interest in participating in the study. This can be a challenge for researchers, who may be in the habit of discussing their research in theoretical terms, whereas a pragmatic, operational presentation may be more effective in convincing key players to take part.

The first contact is critical since it can shape the entire relationship between the investigator and the informants, and therefore can indirectly affect the quality of the data that is collected. Hence the importance of being fully prepared before starting field work. This also applies to inductive research, in which data is gathered from the beginning of the study. Inadequate knowledge of the subject matter can compromise the contact with actors in the field. They often feel they are doing researchers a favour by agreeing to meet with them and listen to what they have to say; informants generally expect investigators to be experts on the subject and to know what they are talking about. The researcher's ability to meet those expectations will determine his or her legitimacy in the eyes of informants and directly affect the information they provide and the longevity of their relationship with the researcher (Hlady Rispal 2002a, b).

 ### Acquire thorough knowledge of the workings of the environment under investigation

The investigator must acquire a sound knowledge of the workings of the environment in which the cases are to be recruited. The support of an individual or organization that already has contacts with the players in this environment can be very useful. To begin with, it helps in identifying potential cases and making first contact in order to determine whether they do meet the sampling criteria. Secondly, it can help induce subjects not only to participate in the study but, even more importantly, to trust the researcher and provide all the required information. The ability to obtain all the information needed for the study is a key factor in choosing a specific case (De Weerd-Nederhof 2001). This can be more problematic in some circles where there is a culture of secrecy, making access more difficult. Some research questions, such as those related to failures, are also perceived as more sensitive than others.

To find cases for my study of business leaders, I turned to the agencies that provide subsidies to Quebec businesses for the introduction of new technologies. As I wanted to observe the technology adoption process from the beginning, I thought companies applying for subsidies would be a suitable pool of potential cases. I met with officials at the agencies to discuss my research with them and explain that my findings might help businesses through the technology adoption process. With assistance from the Association des manufacturiers du Québec, I obtained a list of companies that wanted to introduce new technology, accompanied by a fair amount of corporate information and details on the technology adoption project. The agencies also introduced me to the executives of the businesses I was interested in.

When I found a case that matched my criteria, I had to persuade all the players involved in the project to participate in the study. These included the developer (which could be an outside firm or a department of the company), a funding agency in almost all cases, and of course the business itself, which was obviously the key actor, since I needed the agreement of its owner or senior managers from the outset. Securing their consent was particularly difficult in a period of economic crisis; this is where the support of the funding agencies and the Association des manufacturiers proved most useful.

Another example is a series of case studies of total quality management processes by Sohal, Simon and Lu (1996). They formed a pool of potential subjects using suggestions from faculty colleagues, personal contacts and lists of executives they had met at lectures and conferences. First contact was then made by telephone with the general manager or a plant manager. In this conversation, the study's goals and objectives were explained. The call was followed by a letter in which the research program and the researchers' expectations were described in detail. The researchers report that securing the agreement of the subjects required considerable tact and a good deal of time and effort.

STEP 4.2 Make sure you have no other professional relationship with the subjects

To ensure the impartiality of the study, it is important that the researcher have no professional relationship with the participants other than that related to the study. For example, the investigator should not do a case study of a company for which he or she has worked as a consultant. Neither should the investigator agree to provide professional or other services in exchange for a subject's participation in the study. In many cases, study participants will request some kind of compensation (often they will seek to benefit from the researcher's expertise) in exchange for their time, and this is understandable. There are also subjects who ask to be studied. This can be very attractive to a researcher who is trying to recruit cases, but it increases the risk of absorption or over-assimilation. The investigator may become wound up in the field work and neglect the reflection that is necessary for productive and rigorous research (Hlady Rispal 2002a, b).

STEP 4.3 Consider the geographic distribution of cases

One must always bear in mind that the greater the distance between observation sites and the farther they are from the researcher's home, the more time and money will be required for travel. The challenge, therefore, is to achieve a geographic distribution that satisfies the study's requirements in terms of rigour while enabling the researcher to stay within budget and deadline. This step is particularly important for international research programs that study cases in different countries or even continents.

In my study of business executives, the research sites were spread across the province of Quebec. I had to be very well organized to follow events at each of the sites. It meant I had to be readily available and required a great deal of time, since observation extended over a period of more than two years. We also had to devote fairly large sums of money to travel and accommodation expenses.

 Recruit more than the necessary number of cases

The researcher must safeguard against the risk of mortality during the study, which is to say it may be impossible to observe some cases until the end of the study because they have withdrawn their authorization or for other reasons, such as bankruptcy in the case of companies. Therefore, to make sure the study can proceed to the end, the sample should contain at least one case more than the required minimum.

In our study of medium-sized business executives, the prevailing difficult economic environment made it all the more important to guard against the possibility of losing cases during the study. I therefore observed 12 businesses. Of this number, one was abandoned during the study because it turned out to be a large company, according to our pre-established criteria. The number of employees they had reported was the number they expected to have once the technological changeover was completed, but at the time of the study the company was 150 employees above the 250 maximum established by our size criterion.

Now that the research sites have been selected, we can proceed to the important and delicate data collection stage.

STAGE 5

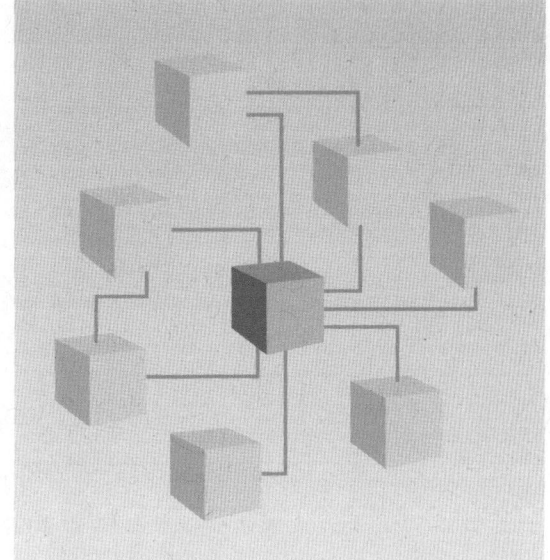

COLLECTING DATA

To assemble rich and credible data in the course of a case study, an investigator must not only be a good observer but also have strong interpersonal skills. Since a case study almost always collects qualitative data, the providers of the data, the informants, are crucially important and the researcher's relationship with them is key. This is not to say that a case study cannot collect quantitative data; for example, in their study of the politics of strategic decision-making in high-velocity environments, Eisenhardt and Bourgeois (1988) developed a questionnaire and administered it to each member of the management team in order to gather quantitative information.

Three rules should be observed when gathering evidence (Yin 2003). First, multiple sources should be used so that the researcher can analyze a variety of information, trace lines of convergence and strengthen construct validity. Secondly, a formal database should be created so that other researchers could, at least in principle, directly review the evidence and verify the study's analyses and conclusions. Thirdly, a chain of evidence should be maintained to ensure consistency and demonstrate the reliability of the data. This chain should also cover the circumstances under which the data was collected. It should therefore be possible for someone from outside the research program to track the evidence all the way from the research question to the conclusions.

There are significant advantages to having several researchers involved in the data gathering process. First, it means there are more resources available for data gathering and the potential for creativity in developing the required tools is increased. More importantly still, convergent observations greatly increase confidence in the collected data (Eisenhardt 1989). However, the lead researcher must coordinate the team, make sure that each team member has harmonious relations with the informants, and see to it that database management is organized in an orderly manner.

Gain acceptance in the research setting

The investigator must establish relations of trust with individuals in each observed setting. The approval of the key player who gave permission for the study does not necessarily guarantee that the other informants approached in the course of the study will be cooperative. If the first contact with each of these individuals is not carefully prepared, they may retreat into bureaucratese and put on an official face in order to present a certain image of themselves to the unknown researcher (Goffman 1959; Hlady Rispal 2002a, b).

The researcher must therefore gain acceptance from the various players in each research setting. This is critically important if we want people to tell us what they really think, because as Whyte (1963: 46) reports, "I found that what people told me helped to explain what had happened and that what I observed helped to explain what people told me." The researcher must be able to inspire confidence and to quickly win credibility in the research setting. At the same time, the investigators must be discreet, not attract attention to themselves, and do nothing to disrupt the dynamics of the phenomenon they want to observe or to change it in any way. This applies to each of the researchers when there are several involved in gathering the evidence. For example Bagchi et al. (1998) report that all members of the research team for their case study of life courses spent two or three days in each locality in order to win the trust of residents.

In my study of medium-sized business executives, some time was invested in developing relationships of trust. At the first meeting with each informant, I introduced myself, took time to discuss my research, and asked whether they had any questions. I then asked about their history with the company and their role in the technology adoption process. Each time I met with them again, I began by asking them how they were doing, even though it was often unrelated to the technology introduction process in which I was interested. This probably accounts for the positive and indeed warm welcome I received from all the subjects I observed, met occasionally or interviewed.

STEP 5.2 Be observant and practice active listening

In order to collect abundant and meaningful evidence, one must be observant and practice active listening. The richest information about informants' experiences with the phenomenon of interest is usually not provided formally or in direct answers to the researcher's questions. Therefore, the investigator must always be alert and avoid presuming what words or deeds will be worthy of attention.

For example, in my study of the behaviour of medium-sized business executives, I did not confine myself to observing the executive behaviour variable, which would have required prior analysis and purging of the collected information; rather, I paid attention to everything that was happening in connection with the technology adoption process.

Active listening means, in practical terms, that in discussions and interviews with informants, the researcher considers not only what they are saying but also what they are feeling. In this sense, listening means more than hearing: it means trying to grasp and understand the hidden meaning and emotions in what is being said. As Boothman (2003: 96) puts it, "You can hear a cello in an orchestra, but listening to that same cello means concentrating on each note and feeling the emotion."

To show they are interested in what the other person is saying, researchers adopt an open, supportive stance, nod, look at the other person. Researchers also use rephrasing to show they understand what is being said. In doing so, they must be careful not to formulate ideas for the informants, or to express their own opinions or emotions. They should tolerate silences and confine themselves to asking questions about points that are not clear to them (Aktouf 1987; Boothman 2003).

STEP 5.3 Use as many information sources as possible

Researchers should identify and use as many sources as possible when gathering data on a case. The goal is not only to collect extensive information but also to ensure that it is an accurate representation of reality. The best way to do so is to compare data collected from

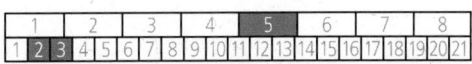

different sources (Benbasat, Goldstein and Mead 1983; Eisenhardt 1989; Lecompte and Goetz 1982; McMillan and Schumacher 1984; Miles 1979; Yin 2003). A number of tests can be performed for this purpose. The most common and effective is probably triangulation, which attempts to systematically check the information collected from one source against at least one and preferably several other sources (Denzin 1978; Jick 1979; Miles and Huberman 1994; Van Maanen 1979; Woodside and Wilson 2003).

In my study of medium-sized business executives, in addition to triangulation I used convergence, tracking, history and other tests to check the consistency of the collected information (Landry, Malouin and Oral 1985).

This is why it is generally accepted that case studies that use several data sources are of better quality than those based on a single source (Yin 2003; Yin, Bateman and Moore 1983). On the other hand, as Yin (1981a) notes, the greatest challenge facing the researcher who chooses to use the case method for research is dealing with the many sources of evidence. To meet this challenge, the investigator must master each of the different data collection procedures.

The six leading data collection techniques used in case studies are, in order of required degree of involvement in the research setting, participant observation, non-participant or direct observation, interviews, documentation, archives and physical artefacts (Yin 2003; Webb et al. 1999; Schatzman and Strauss 1973; Murphy 1980). Here is a brief description of each.

Participant Observation

In participant observation, the investigator plays a role in the observed situation and participates directly in the events, especially in the case of anthropological studies. This can give us access to events that would otherwise be beyond the reach of scientific examination and enable us to see reality from the standpoint of someone within the situation. It should be borne in mind, however, that participant observation can raise serious issues that must be addressed, most notably ethical questions and problems of analytic bias (Becker 1958; Yin 2003).

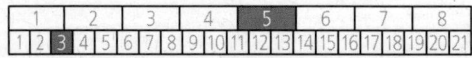

Non-participant or Direct Observation

Non-participant observation is used to gather evidence on observable behaviours or situations. It can range from formal data collection based on an observation protocol (measuring a specific behaviour during defined periods of time in a specified place) to an informal approach in which every visit is an opportunity for spontaneous data collection. Clearly, having more than one observer enhances the reliability of observations of this type, as does taking photographs or even filming the activities (Yin 2003; Dabbs 1982).

Interviews

Interviews are among the most important sources of information. Interviews can be classified into three types, based on two criteria: the amount of leeway granted the respondent and the degree of depth or detail. In an open-ended interview, a central theme is given as a topic for discussion and simply broken down into a few pre-determined sub-themes. The respondent leads the interview. The researcher must avoid becoming overly dependent on the information the respondent provides: everything that is said should be corroborated with other sources. In a semi-structured interview, the interviewer asks precise questions, somewhat reducing the amount of freedom enjoyed by the respondents but still allowing them considerable leeway. The interviewer still asks open-ended questions but with more structured content, as the questions are based on certain typical themes drawn from the research protocol. Finally, in a structured interview, a series of structured questions are asked. This type of interview can amount to an orally administered questionnaire. In this case, sampling and statistical analysis can be applied to the collected data (Aktouf 1987; Yin 2003; Pinto and Grawitz 1969).

An interview should be considered a verbal report subject to problems of bias. The greater the leeway allowed to the respondent, the more important it is to corroborate the responses using other information sources. Taping the interview can help enhance the reliability of the analysis but can be inappropriate in some circumstances. For example, the respondent may refuse, or feel uncomfortable; there may be no systematic transcription or listening procedure planned; the interviewer's fussing with the tape recorder may be disturbing; or the taping may make the researcher feel that active listening is not necessary (Aktouf 1987; Yin 2003).

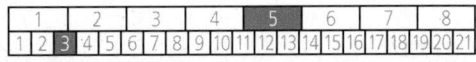

Documentation

Documentation includes letters, press releases, media publications, and other written materials that may not necessarily be precise or free of bias but can serve to corroborate information from other sources (Yin 2003).

Archives

Archives can include memos, personal notes, cards or lists of names. Unlike documentation, researchers must check the origin and accuracy of each of these documents, interpret them, and use only the ones they consider relevant to their study (Yin 2003).

Physical Artefacts

Physical artefacts can take various forms: technical procedures, tools, instruments, works of art, etc. They are not appropriate for all case studies but they can sometimes be an important component of the information set.

The researcher uses some or all of these information sources to assemble a database that may contain documents, statistical data (questionnaires or other quantitative data), narrative material (interview report, tape, etc.) and also the researcher's notes, which are very important. Field notes can take various forms and include different types of content: they may provide a faithful description of what the researcher saw, heard, felt, etc., or contain methodological comments, i.e., the researcher's messages to oneself on the data gathering process (who to talk to, what to wear, when to call, etc.), theoretical observations (ideas, hypotheses, criticisms or reflections), descriptions of the feelings prompted by the study or the subjects, or the researcher's uncensored doubts, disappointments and hopes (Richardson 1994). Van Maanen (1988) describes field notes as "an ongoing stream-of-consciousness commentary" on the progress of the study. They will be highly useful, if not indispensable, when the time comes to draw connections between data collection, analysis and interpretation (De Weerd-Nederhof 2001; Eisenhardt 1989).

To monitor each technology adoption process on an ongoing basis for my study of medium-sized business executives, I was in weekly communication, preferably through face-to-face meetings, with the developer. During the meetings, I found out about completed

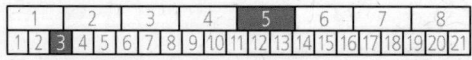

and planned actions for each technology adoption process, the actors involved and the developer's perception of the progress of the process. It was also at these meetings that we decided which activities I would participate in on-site.

At the sites, I met with the company's employees, regardless of their level in the organization, and I experienced, to some extent, the real-life situations associated with each technology adoption process. Immediately after each meeting or observation visit, I wrote a report using a predefined model.

In the course of the study, I also performed a thorough analysis of all the written documentation on each project. This documentation consisted primarily in studies of various types, exchanges of correspondence, and technical or administrative texts. I was then equipped to discuss the content of the documents with the informants and confirm that my understanding of the texts was correct. Finally, in the last phase of observation or afterwards, I held a more formal meeting/interview with senior managers at each company.

In my field notes, I wrote down literally every thought that entered my head before, during and after the data collection sessions. I recorded comments on the conduct of each data collection session, methodological remarks, my thoughts or intuitions about the informants and the data analysis and so forth, on a form with the following headings: observation conditions, executive's behaviour, comments on informant, data collected, data collection context, data collection technique, preliminary conclusions, and other comments.

STEP 5.4 Fine-tune the data collection strategy

In the preparatory stage, a preliminary version of the data collection strategy, including the data collection technique and an outline of the data coding scheme, was produced. Now that the specific cases to be studied have been selected and the researcher has acquired cursory knowledge of each site and established contacts with informants, the data collection strategy needs to be fine-tuned and adapted to each case. The data collection instruments should also be developed or finalized at this stage.

Data collection instruments and techniques should generally be flexible and adapted to the situation at each site. The investigator is always free to modify the data gathering techniques or instruments

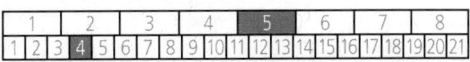

in the course of the study, or even to add new ones (De Weerd-Nederhof 2001; Eisenhardt 1989). This being said, data collection does need to be guided by a protocol. This is particularly important in view of the wide range of sources used. The protocol should define the focus of the study and what types of evidence are relevant. It may also set the minimum quantity of data required from an operational point of view (Yin 1981a).

On this basis, it is now possible to make sampling decisions for each case and determine which individuals, sites and events will be observed. Once again, experience and intuition suggest we should seek a sample that is diverse rather then representative, while taking into account issues of accessibility and the time each case will require (Stake 1994). All operational aspects of the various information collection techniques that will be used must also be determined. For example, if participant observation is to be used, one must decide what role the investigator will play (how, when, for how long). In the case of non-participant observation, we must answer the questions when, how, for how long, at what intervals, for which specific events. In the case of interviews, we need to know the type, the length, with whom, where, the topics and questions. Strategies for ensuring the reliability and validity of the collected evidence must also be selected. These are all decisions that must be made in the data collection strategy fine-tuning stage (Aktouf 1987).

In their published article on their life course study, Bagchi et al. (1998) report that they decided to use semi-structured interviews. They conducted the number of interviews with community members that they needed in order to be able to properly describe common life-change processes and situations.

For their case study of the politics of strategic decision-making in high-velocity environments, Eisenhardt and Bourgeois (1988) decided to interview each executive and administer a questionnaire to each member of the management team as well. They also agreed that, to ensure validity, each of the interviews would be carried out by a team of two researchers, one of whom would conduct the interview while the other would take notes and fill in any gaps and that immediately after the interview the two researchers would check the facts and write down their individual impressions.

In a study of quality management best practices in Australian service industries, Sohal, Simon and Lu (1996) not only made several visits to each company under investigation but visited different

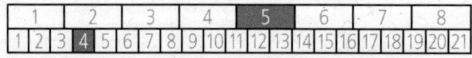

company sites: plants, offices, warehouses, stores. They collected documents including annual reports, instruction manuals, procedural manuals, corporate work charts, and so forth.

In my study of the behaviour of medium-sized business executives, after collecting evidence through direct observation, I decided to meet more formally with senior managers at each company. Of course, I had had discussions with these executives throughout the observation process, but it seemed to me that a semi-structured interview would serve two purposes: probing the behaviour of the executives in the technology introduction process and testing the main conclusions I had drawn from my observations and discussions.

The researcher must also make sure, particularly when there are several people collecting field data, that the data is consistent and that the data collected by different people is systematically comparable (Miles 1979). As well, precautions must be taken in the event that informants disappear in the course of the study before providing full information on their experience in connection with the phenomenon of interest, which is always a possibility.

 **STEP 5.5** ## Develop a data definition table and a chain of evidence

Throughout the field observation process, we must build a data definition table and a chain of evidence for the collected data and keep them up to date in order to maintain some consistency in the meanings assigned to the data. This bolsters reliability by enabling an outside observer to follow the trail of evidence from the research question to the conclusions, see all the stages leading from the former to the latter, trace and understand the quotes in the research report from segments of the database, and determine the circumstances under which the information was gathered (Yin 2003).

Keeping a log of events and observations made during each field session is one way to produce the data definition table and chain of evidence (Richardson 1994). The investigator's notes, as described above, can also be entered in the database.

In my study of medium-sized business executives and new technologies, I checked the content of my records with the relevant informants. In this way, I was able to ascertain that the meaning I attached to the evidence was the same as that ascribed by the informants, and that this meaning survived the changes in respondents in

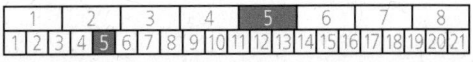

the course of the study. As noted above, I also used a standard form that I filled out after every field visit, entering notes on the meaning and significance of the collected data.

Manage the data

The researcher must manage the collected evidence in a highly structured and orderly way, and keep it secure. The database quickly grows to substantial size and considerable diversity, particularly when the study covers several cases. Data management will be key to the quality of data analysis and interpretation: the accuracy of the results depends on it.

Being very flexible on the type and form of the evidence we are collecting should never be a reason for not being systematic – quite the contrary (Eisenhardt 1989; De Weerd-Nederhof 2001; Yin 2003). Each piece of data must be carefully identified: information such as the case to which it applies, the informant, the date on which it was collected, the circumstances and so forth should be recorded. The researcher should also record any comments on an attached note as soon as possible after the data was collected in order to ensure the reliability of the information. The evidence on each case should be placed in one file to enable organized follow-up and to make it possible for the researcher to refresh his or her memory by consulting the file before doing more work on the case.

For reasons of security, a full copy of the database should be stored in a different location if possible. Electronic files should be backed up frequently and stored in a safe place.

In my study of the behaviour of medium-sized business executives, there was a large number of study sites and they were far apart. A good deal of organization was required in order to keep tabs on activities at each of the sites. The direct observation process also extended over a period of more than two years and for each case data was collected on several occasions. Obviously, the amount and variety of the collected data made it necessary to spend an enormous amount of time on identification, classification and follow-up. Each document in the database was also photocopied and the copy was stored at my home. Electronic files were backed up weekly and stored in a locked filing cabinet.

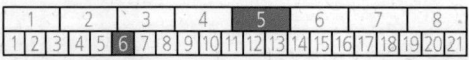

STEP 5.7   Make a smooth exit

In a case study, the investigator is in regular contact with the subjects over an extended period of time, establishing a relationship that can be quite close and even intense: a qualitative case study requires the researcher to spend a considerable amount of time at the site following the informants and the activities. The researcher is therefore admitted into a private space (Stake 1994); he must be on his best behaviour and follow a strict code of ethics.

When the time comes for the researcher to end the relationship, he should do so without disrupting the environment, leaving as he came, quietly, without leaving an imprint on the research setting. Often, there will be a formal leave-taking, or the researcher may send a letter thanking the informants for their help and informing them of the project's future course. One must be very careful in discussing follow-up and mention only what can and will be done, for it is a serious matter for researchers to make promises they will not keep.

The leave-taking is important both for expressing gratitude to the participants in the study and for projecting a positive image of the researcher, so that informants at each site will have a receptive attitude towards other researchers who may seek their participation in future studies.

In my study of the behaviour of medium-sized business executives, as I was present in the organizational environments where the new technologies were being introduced and numerous people confided in me, I followed standard ethical procedures (Canada Council 1977; Diener and Crandall 1977). For example, I made specific commitments, often in writing, to keep the information I was given confidential. In many cases, I had or could have access to trade secrets. Some of the executives therefore insisted that none of their competitors be included in the study. Some even asked me to give my word that I did not and would not have any contacts with any of their competitors. They all asked me to guarantee that their company would be kept anonymous in all written or verbal reports on the study. I was very careful to keep those commitments to the letter.

After the highly organized and structured data collection process, it can be a relief to proceed to the next stage, the analysis of the data.

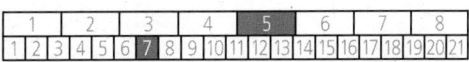

STAGE 6

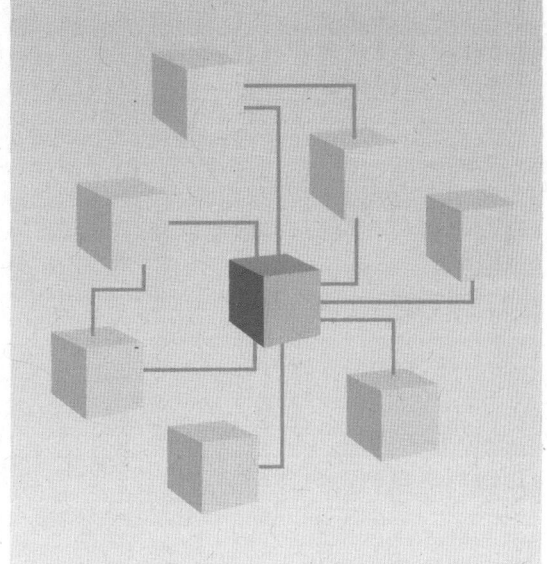

ANALYZING DATA

I should point out to begin with that although I am describing this stage after the data collection stage, it is always preferable to carry out the two iteratively. It can be a serious mistake to devote oneself exclusively to data collection for a time and then go home and start analyzing the data, especially if the study is breaking new theoretical ground. At that stage, it can be difficult if not impossible to go back into the field to fill in gaps or test new hypotheses that suggest themselves in the course of the analysis (Huberman and Miles 1991).

During the data collection process, researchers begin discerning the meaning of the information: they note patterns, trends, possible explanations and ways of arranging the data. These meanings that emerge from the evidence must be tested: are they credible, solid, certain – in a word, are they valid (Huberman and Miles 1991)? When several researchers are involved in the project, team meetings provide an opportunity to tie together the data collection and analysis process. Having a research team allows for greater flexibility in data gathering (Eisenhardt 1989; Glaser and Strauss 1967). Of course, it can also complicate the researcher's job, insofar as team interactions can make the data gathering and analysis stages more demanding and stressful (Miles 1979).

In the data collection stage, the researcher builds a database, usually consisting of qualitative data. The evidence may have been gathered in different ways and may not be highly structured, but still it is made up of words, usually organized into text (Huberman and Miles 1991). To process this database, the researcher must go back and forth between three concurrent activities: purging, coding and analyzing the data (De Weerd-Nederhof 2001; Miles and Huberman 1994).

 **STEP 6.1 Purge the collected data**

We must make sure our evidence is relevant to the study, that it is in an appropriate format for coding, and that we have the required basic information on its source and how it was collected. A preliminary review should also be performed of each item to make sure its content really is related to the object of study. We must also make sure the format of the data is compatible with the planned coding strategy and tools. For example, if a software has been chosen, it must be possible to enter the documents and texts in the database.

One might think that collecting and recording data in a predetermined format will save time, but this is not necessarily true. Not only might this approach fail to yield the desired benefits, but it can also diminish the richness of the evidence. A qualitative database is a work in progress: as new data is added, it complements, clarifies, informs and may even disqualify the previous data (Huberman and Miles 1991).

In my study of medium-sized business executives, a number of documents were eventually eliminated because they dealt only with technical aspects of the technology, such as programming or systems architecture.

 **STEP 6.2 Code the collected data**

The first thing that needs to be done is to organize and classify the data to make it easier to analyze. More precisely, we need to identify information units that relate directly to the phenomenon of interest (Catterall and Maclaran 1996; Huberman and Miles 1991; Tesch 1990). This is where it becomes important to have a previously developed coding system in order to systematize this critical and highly delicate process (Huberman and Miles 1991; Miles 1979). The data coding and classification process consists in identifying and coding passages in the texts that describe or relate to categories or concepts connected to the phenomenon of interest. It is then possible to classify the data, grouping together items that belong to the same category. While there are still researchers who do not use this coding/classification method, it is the most widely recommended approach to managing rich and complex evidence (Richards and Richards 1994).

More concretely, to code a text we begin by reading it through very carefully several times in order to familiarize ourselves with its content and general meaning (Aktouf 1987). The text is then broken down into units of information, each of which is assigned a code. The units should be the smallest items that can be assigned to one category or another. This could be a word, a sentence, a general idea or a full passage describing an experience related to the phenomenon of interest (Bachelor and Joshi 1986).

The categories into which the information units will be organized may be defined using one of two methods. In the top-down approach, used mainly in education and cognitive psychology, the investigator starts from a set of principles, laws and concepts, and then attempts to glean the meaning of the text and establish the categories on the basis of these pre-existing notions (Boje 1991; Heise 1992). In the bottom-up approach, which is widely used in ethnographic research, the researcher starts from the information units in the texts to develop a system of categories that can help describe or explain the phenomenon under study (Manning and Cullum-Swan 1994). In this case, the investigator needs to be even more systematic so as not to omit any possible categories.

Once a category has been defined, we must consider whether it adds something new to the description of the phenomenon, and if so whether it is the only category that can serve the purpose. One should avoid having too few categories that are overly rigid or closed, or on the contrary too many categories that are overly detailed or subdivided (Aktouf 1987).

It is therefore a mistake to think that the coding and classification process can get in the way of theory-building. The challenge is to adapt the coding/classification method in order to record, connect, explore, test and cumulatively build up the information that is extracted from the data. The researcher weaves together the ideas, concepts and categories that emerge from the evidence in order to develop a theory (Richards and Richards 1994).

This process can be carried out manually: identifying the information units in a text by making margin notes is a form of coding (Richards and Richards 1994). But this approach can become cumbersome if the database is large and/or covers several cases. Moreover, as the manual coding and recoding process proceeds, there can be a strong tendency to make the evidence fit the categories. It should also be noted that a segment of text may be assigned more than one code,

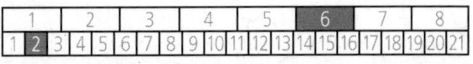

although this practice is not advisable in manual coding as it makes analysis complicated and unwieldy (Catterall and Maclaran 1996; Miles and Huberman 1994).

It is not surprising, therefore, that researchers soon discovered the usefulness of computers for qualitative research (Seidel and Clark 1982). First, the word processor replaced the typewriter. Drass (1980, 1989) showed that the computer could be harnessed to perform mechanical aspects of qualitative analysis without compromising methodological soundness (Seidel and Clark 1984). But regardless of the coding method used, we must realize that defining the categories and deciding how each unit of information should be classified cannot be a series of clerical decisions. If an electronic tool is used, the "garbage in, garbage out" rule must be borne in mind. The richness of the data analysis will be directly influenced by the soundness of the decisions made when coding the content of the texts (Richards and Richards 1994). Intellectual tasks must remain the purview of the researcher, although it has been argued that computers can assist the process (Catterall and Maclaran 1996; Dey 1993; Richards and Richards 1991; Weitzman and Miles 1995).

Without describing in detail all the software available on the market, it may be useful to say a few words on this subject here. Using a computer for data analysis can have a considerable impact on the research process. The impact may be positive, opening up new possibilities, or negative, introducing stifling restrictions into the data analysis process (Richards and Richards 1994).

It is possible to use qualitative data analysis software only for coding and classification. However, these applications can do much more: by providing easy access to data, they can be used to support activities such as defining descriptive categories, exploring underlying patterns or developing and testing hypotheses (Bogdan and Taylor 1975; Richards and Richards 1994). They can also be used for triangulation since they make it much easier to compare text segments from different sources.

There are several types of qualitative data analysis support applications (Richards and Richards 1994). Starting with the most basic, in terms of the range of relevant functions they support, there are word processors, which make it possible to search a text and insert hyperlinks. Their usefulness is confined to evidence that consists of words, such as interview transcripts, and is formatted as a text document. Their main limitation is that they do not support grouping of similarly coded passages.

There are also full-text search engines, which can search a number of files, even if they are not open. These also support fast keyword searching and can generate statistics on a variety of co-occurrences. They are very helpful for channelling the researcher's intuitions and enable the researcher to play around with the evidence, experimentally coding a large body of words and sentences, and chopping up the texts in different ways (Catterall and Maclaran 1996; Dey 1993; Richards and Richards 1991; Tesch 1990; Weitzman and Miles 1995).

Relational database software is much more sophisticated: it can be used to manage the collected data and also to analyze it. The advantage of this type of application is primarily that it supports functions such as sorting records entered in numerical, Boolean or text fields, or a combination of the three, filtering records, or extracting records with a specified value. A database of this type is called relational because the investigator can relate one table to another, provided there is a common field. However, to use this type of software effectively, the research team may need to have an IT specialist with a background in database design.

Some researchers have reservations about using electronic tools for qualitative data analysis (Catterall and Maclaran 1996). They raise a number of points that researchers should consider before deciding to do so. First, there is a danger that the study design will be unduly influenced by the features of the software the researcher is familiar with or wants to use (Agar 1991). It takes a good deal of time to master a new research support application, which can spur researchers to use software with which they are already familiar, even if it is not entirely appropriate in view of the research design (Tesch 1990). It should also be noted that many of these applications are designed for the grounded-theory approach (Fielding 1993) and often focus on analysis of variables rather than analysis of cases *per se* (Miles and Huberman 1994).

When it comes to data coding and analysis, these applications lend themselves to detailed and often complex coding structures, which can lead researchers to get bogged down in this step. There is also a fear that data analysis will become mechanical rather than creative and that the features of the software will condition the type of analysis that is performed (Bryman and Burgess 1994; Dey 1993).

More importantly still, there is a danger of losing the richness and complexity of the data when it is processed and analyzed in isolation from the full original text (Catterall and Maclaran 1996). It is therefore important to make sure that use of these electronic tools does not

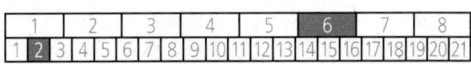

distance the investigator from the evidence (Seidel 1991) or serve to increase the quantity of data processed at the expense of the quality of the analysis (Catterall and Maclaran 1996; Seidel 1991).

Though software developers have given us a spate of revolutionary applications, none of the products currently available matches the needs of qualitative research exactly and fully. The subtler and more intuitive aspects of the way the human mind processes information are probably the most exciting part of qualitative research, but they are also the most difficult to reproduce on a computer. The intricate and elaborate work of deriving meaning from the evidence is and probably always will be up to the researcher. This being said, there is no question that electronic tools facilitate the process by streamlining the mechanical component of the task and increasing the amount of evidence the researcher can analyze (Richards and Richards 1994; Seidel and Clark 1984).

In my study of medium-sized business executives, the detailed comparison chart of entrepreneurial and administrative behaviour developed by Stevenson (1983, 1984, 1986) was used as the basis for the coding system. Stevenson's model describes and analyzes differences in behaviour in five dimensions. All the collected documents on each case were coded using this model. I manually identified and coded each unit of information that seemed related to any of the model's five dimensions.

STEP 6.3 Analyze the coded data

The researcher must listen to data to see if any patterns emerge, i.e. whether evidence from different sources converges towards similar conclusions (Yin 1981a). To do so, the investigator must get immersed in the evidence, in the configuration of the facts and the interconnections. Researchers must strive to avoid becoming overly excited about preliminary interpretations, as this can lead them to slant the subsequent analysis to support their initial thesis (Hlady Rispal 2002a, b; Miles and Huberman 1994). This is probably the most difficult step in conducting a case study and the one that is most neglected in the literature (Eisenhardt 1989).

At this point, the researcher will generally have a body of evidence that speaks to him or her, and ways of approaching the information will suggest themselves. However, it is best to let the data

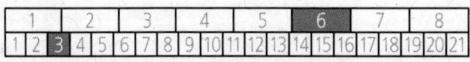

percolate a while, to take the time to reread it several times, re-examine it, allow connections to take shape and an overall picture to emerge. Producing a detailed description of each case is key to generating intuitions (Gersick 1988). This step necessarily involves a certain amount of trial and error, which can be frustrating (Eisenhardt 1989).

This within-case analysis should be accompanied by a cross-case analysis in order to identify patterns. The cross-case analysis can be performed by first selecting categories or dimensions and then looking at within-group and cross-group differences and similarities. It is also possible to select case pairs and list differences and similarities between the two cases, and then between pairs of cases (Eisenhardt 1989).

As we have said, the evidence we are analyzing consists of words embedded in texts of varying lengths and taken from different sources. Content analysis, a method of detailed document examination, is therefore a highly useful technique to use at this stage. Content analysis helps reveal what the content has to say about the phenomenon of interest and generates what has been referred to as "knowledge deduced from content" (Bardin 1996). Its purpose is to show meanings, associations and intentions that may not be evident on a straight reading of the document. Content analysis proceeds through a systematic, quantitative, objective description of the explicit content of the documents under analysis. It is systematic in the sense that all the content of all the documents is analyzed, organized and integrated; quantitative insofar as we count meaningful elements in order to make calculations, statistical comparisons, weightings, frequency analyses, etc.; and objective in the sense that another investigator analyzing the same data using the same method and with the same purpose should arrive at roughly the same conclusions (Aktouf 1987; Bardin 1996; Berelson 1952; Clandinin 1994; Kracauer 1993; Lécuyer 1987; Manning and Cullum-Swan 1994; Pinto and Grawitz 1969; Rubin and Rubin 1995).

Either verbal or written texts can be subjected to content analysis. The documents may consist of so-called naturally occurring data or researcher-provoked data. The former is data produced by humans for purposes of communication; the second is data created for the purposes of the study, based on observation, questionnaires, investigations, interviews and so forth (Aktouf 1987; Bardin 1996).

Content analysis generally consists of three stages. The first two, coding and classifying the content of the texts, are described in the discussion of the previous step. The third is analysis *per se:* the

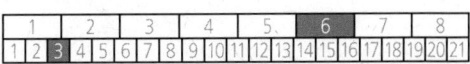

researcher dissects the texts using the predetermined categories and counts the occurrences of each element to determine their frequency. Inductive conclusions can then be drawn from the evidence, which is the ultimate goal of content analysis. The weighted frequency of the information units or categories can be compared, using statistical tests or other methods. Identifying the most prominent patterns in the evidence by this method can be immensely useful for describing, explaining and understanding the phenomenon of interest.

Of course, mathematical processing of information units and categories is greatly facilitated by the computer. Once the data has been coded, almost any of the appropriate applications can be used to search for segments by code, keyword or a combination of search criteria, using the Boolean logical operators "AND," "OR" and "NOT." There are limitations to the use of this function, however, as the codes relate more to the meaning of the text segment than to its content as such (Catterall and Maclaran 1996).

These computer applications can automatically assemble all segments with the same code and indicate the source of each segment. Other applications perform direct full-text searches. For example, *Metamorph*, which is considered one of the most powerful (Weitzman and Miles 1995), does not use Boolean operators but rather semantic relationships, letting the investigator query the database using natural language (Shapiro et al. 1993). It can search not only for words and sentences but also synonyms, fuzzy matches and even spelling mistakes.

This type of quantitative analysis is certainly a significant indicator of a pattern but others must also be considered. Just because an information unit or category ranks low in the frequency count does not mean it should be dismissed. Other indicators should also be analyzed: for example, breaking down the data by source may increase the weight of some points, which have been corroborated by several informants (Eisenhardt 1989). The content of the information units and categories must also be assessed to determine whether they should be checked again in the field. Here again, we see the importance of collecting and analyzing the evidence on an iterative basis.

This analysis may also reveal contradictory evidence. The investigator's first, often involuntary, reflex is to dismiss or ignore it. A few pieces of counter-evidence can be enough to threaten the whole system. The researcher may therefore be reluctant to recognize them and may gloss them over without being aware of it. Others regard counter-evidence as an opportunity to improve their understanding

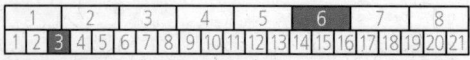

of the data. In this case, we must be careful to avoid the opposite risk of overestimating the importance of the contradictory evidence, which is also liable to skew the results. Other issues of a more technical nature may also arise, since the contradictory data may be the result of different data gathering methods or mistaken application of techniques (Hlady Rispal 2002a, b).

We must therefore consider, first of all, whether the contradictory evidence may be due to shortcomings in the data gathering *modus operandi.* If not, we must then probe deeper to check the data again and try to explain the contradictions. If, after double-checking, the counter-evidence still stands, it must be taken into account and reflected in the findings.

In my study of medium-sized business executives, I tried to identify patterns, convergences and other possible observations through an inductive analysis of the coded body of evidence. I first looked at each case individually. Then I performed a comparative analysis of all the cases. I used triangulation extensively to ascertain the degree of agreement between different sources.

For each of the five dimensions in Stevenson's model, I produced a table showing the characteristics of each case in terms of that dimension. I then produced a summary table showing all the cases. That made the analysis of cross-case convergences easier to perform and, most importantly, easier for other researchers reviewing my study to check. I was then able to situate each case on the entre-preneurial/administrative behaviour continuum for each of Stevenson's five dimensions. The result was five charts such as the one below.

Chart 3
Distribution of Cases by Commitment to Opportunity

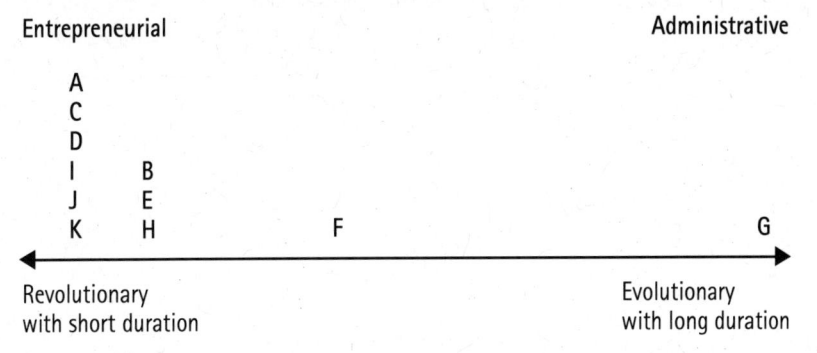

STEP 6.4   Write a description of each case

The purpose of this step is, in the first instance, to organize the evidence that supports the patterns identified in the analysis into a narrative, and most importantly to elaborate on these patterns by returning them to their specific context. Not only is this contextualization useful for validating the results of the data analysis, but it is also essential for guiding the interpretation that will be developed in the next stage. As we have noted, computer tools lead the researcher to work with the data out of context, and content analysis also fails to consider the frame within which a document is meaningful (Manning and Cullum-Swan 1994).

Writing a case description is, first and foremost, a rhetorical process. It proceeds from the results of the data analysis that was performed in light of the research problem and questions. The observed patterns in the categories, concepts and constructs must be presented, using the information units identified in the analysis, supported with arguments, and placed in the specific context of each case (Hlady Rispal 2002a, b). One must report not only the events related to the phenomenon of interest but also contextual elements. These may be information on the organization, its history and its people, or on the origins and development of the phenomenon. Much like an ethnographic narrative, the description should make generous use of quotes to be faithful to the evidence and so the informants can relate to it.

The writing style should combine the rigour of the theoretician with the elegance of a popularizer who wants to make his or her findings readily understandable. One must take care not to oversimplify, nor on the contrary to produce a dense and abstract text that is impenetrable for common mortals, a frequent pitfall for researchers who are determined to render the full richness and interconnectedness of all the evidence they have gathered and analyzed (Hlady Rispal 2002a, b). For ethical reasons, this description must not refer explicitly to any statements made by any identifiable informant. When individuals must be identified, their titles should be used rather than their names.

Some sources (Stake 1995; Van Maanen 1988) make no distinction between the case description and the research report. However, the research report is intended for a scholarly audience and

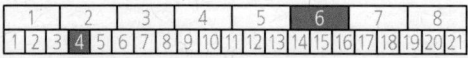

includes not only the description of the case but other matter such as the methodology, mechanisms for ensuring the accuracy of the results, the interpretation of the evidence, and so forth (Hlady Rispal 2002a, b).

On the other hand, the case description is intended to be submitted to the informants, who are asked to comment on whether the document reflects reality. This is a delicate process, for the description may be quite displeasing to them. It is advisable to begin by explaining to informants how the study progressed, i.e., the patterns that emerged from the data analysis process. The idea is neither to support one point of view over another nor to reproduce the testimony of one informant in particular. It should be made clear to informants at the outset that this is a factual description of events and of the context surrounding the phenomenon of interest: the investigator is not taking sides. It is also a good idea to warn informants that they may be surprised, disappointed or even shocked by the document. The continuation of the process should then be explained to the informants: they should be advised that their comments on the content of the description will be taken into account if they can be supported with facts or confirmed by the collected evidence.

Sohal, Simon and Lu (1996) proceeded in this manner in their study of quality management best practices in Australian service industries. Their article reports that they wrote a description of each case and sent it to the organization's executives not only for fact-checking purposes but also to secure their approval of the content for publication with their research findings.

In my research on medium-sized business executives, I prepared a separate history of each case of technology introduction that I studied. To make the text more readable and avoid weighing it down with subheadings, I used the same outline for each history: first a description of the company and its management structure, which corresponds to the fifth dimension in Stevenson's model, then a description of the technology that was adopted, and finally my data on the other four dimensions in Stevenson's model (strategic orientation, commitment to opportunity, the resource commitment process, and control over resources).

As I had given each company an ironclad guarantee of confidentiality and anonymity, I had to be very careful and often less forthcoming than I would have liked to be with the information I had been given. However, the information I withheld had no direct bearing

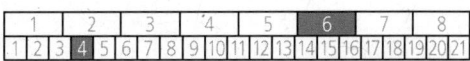

on the conclusions of the analysis. For example, in one case I could not report the company's location and line of business, which would have made it readily identifiable.

We shall now turn to the last stage in conducting a case study: interpreting the data once it has been coded and analyzed.

STAGE 7

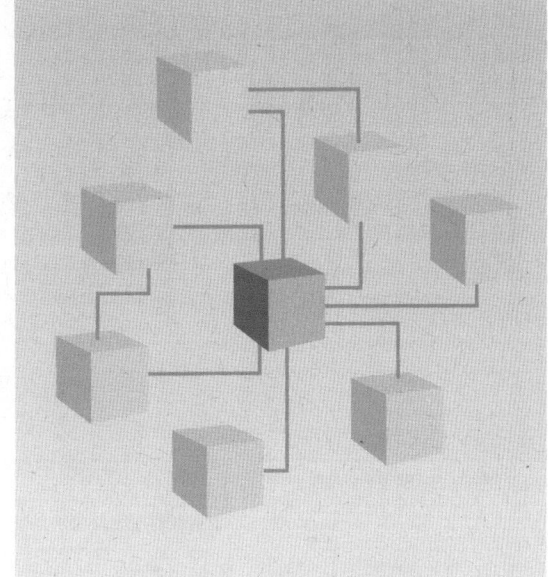

INTERPRETING
DATA

n the data interpretation stage, the investigator's creativity and imagination come into play. Researchers must harness their intuitive understanding to explain the phenomenon of interest. To do so, they should review the evidence at a higher level of abstraction and interpret it to extract the meanings they have deduced from the characteristics and patterns identified in the data analysis stage (Bardin 1996; Yin 2003). There is an important distinction between the preceding stage, data analysis, in which coding, classification and analysis techniques were applied to the content of the texts, and the more conceptual data interpretation stage, in which theoretical approaches to reality are applied (Richards and Richards 1994).

The interpretive process pursues reality but can never fully reveal it. What it can do is to mine knowledge that is potentially translatable into action (Wacheux 2002). It draws analogies with a view to producing tested, plausible theoretical explanations of the phenomenon under study. These explanations are developed gradually through a complex effort of idea generation, comparison and verification. The three activities are conducted simultaneously as part of an interconnected, incremental, iterative process (Hlady Rispal 2002a, b).

STEP 7.1 Generate proposed explanations

Coming up with possible explanations is probably the most delicate and demanding part of the case study, for it relies primarily on the investigator's creativity and intuition. The challenge is to find a plausible conceptual explanation for the phenomenon of interest (Eisenhardt 1989; Glaser and Strauss 1967; Hlady Rispal 2002a, b; Stake 1994).

As we have said, using the case study as a research method can shed new light on a phenomenon by developing or testing a theory. The final product may therefore be a concept, such as Mintzberg and Waters' (1982) "deliberate" and "emergent" strategies, a conceptual framework, as in Harris and Sutton's (1986) study of bankruptcy, or theoretical proposals (Eisenhardt and Bourgeois 1988; Hlady Rispal 2002a, b). These novel ideas are referred to as new theories but they are developed by incorporating, exploring and building on existing theories, particularly when the aim of the study is to test one theory in particular (Richards and Richards 1994). The core of the interpretation process is an ongoing comparison of the new theory with the evidence for the purpose of producing a theoretical explanation of each case in its local context (Eisenhardt 1989; Wacheux 2002; Yin 2003).

To generate these ideas, concepts, hypotheses or theoretical proposals with the potential to explain the phenomenon under investigation, researchers have two main approaches available to them. First, they can revisit the preliminary stages of the process: they can go back to the definition of the research problem produced in the "assessing appropriateness" stage, review the definition of the research question in the "preparation" stage, reread the conclusions they drew at the time, or turn for inspiration to their original explanatory hypotheses and assumptions.

It is often possible to refine these concepts and constructs in the interpretation stage. The investigator may wish to review relevant indicators for each case. More often than not, the definitions of the constructs and particularly their measurement emerge from the data analysis and interpretation process. In a case study, factorial analysis can be used to combine several indicators into a single measure of a construct. Many researchers therefore use tables to systematically summarize the underlying data (Miles and Huberman 1984; Sutton and Callahan 1987; Yin 2003).

The second – and probably most important – approach available to researchers for generating explanatory ideas, particularly if the purpose of the case study is theory-building, is to apply their creativity and intuition. To do so, the researcher can start from the detailed description of each case and ponder its deeper meaning, consider the collected data and the associated patterns from a more conceptual point of view, develop his or her impressions of these points, summarize them, and produce an overview (Richards and Richards 1994). This process prompts the investigator to search the evidence for new meanings and ideas, achieve a better understanding of a perception, behaviour or situation, and arrive at a description or explanation of the phenomenon of interest (Hlady Rispal 2002a, b).

To apprehend the phenomena and the causal relationships at a more abstract level, it is often useful to distinguish the particular from the general in order to subsume the former under the latter, and to identify the dependent, independent and moderating variables to determine possible relationships among them. The investigator may also attempt to establish causal relationships to help explain the phenomenon of interest, although these are fairly complex and difficult to measure with precision when working with qualitative data (Wacheux 2002; Yin 2003).

In my study of business executives and technology adoption, a number of important points emerged from the process of defining the research problem. First, market demand and the inherent attraction of the technology worked together to motivate businesses to migrate to new technologies. But the decision-makers faced structural, technical and human barriers to making the change. Secondly, there was a management model for the technology adoption process that provided managers with tools to help them overcome these barriers and successfully introduce the new technology at the company. Thirdly, this model was based on a planning approach and assigned the executive a critical role. Fourth, the case studies found in the literature showed that the executives were more inclined to use a trial-and-error approach to managing the technology adoption process. Fifth, executives could take two quite different approaches to the technology adoption process: entrepreneurial or administrative. Sixth, executives of small and medium-sized businesses were more likely to take an entrepreneurial approach and the rate of technology adoption was lower at those firms. Seventh, Stevenson had found significant differences between entrepreneurial and administrative behaviour in terms of five core dimensions: strategic orientation, commitment to opportunity, the resource commitment process, control over resources and management.

The development of the research question was informed by these points. It became clear to me that the question was two-pronged. First, given that there was a motivation to migrate to new

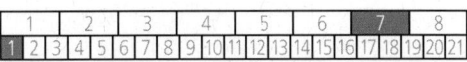

technologies and a technology adoption management model capable of overcoming the barriers to adoption was available, why was the rate of new technology penetration at the companies still relatively low? Second, why was it that in practice the executives managed the technology adoption process by trial and error when there was a well-documented planning model available that could guarantee a smoother and more successful migration, enabling the company to leverage the full potential of the new technology?

As the top executive plays a critical role in the technology adoption process, Stevenson's distinction between entrepreneurial and administrative behaviour appeared relevant. It would have been logical to assume that both the executives' motivations and the planning model for managing the technology adoption process would fall into the administrative category. However, my hypothesis was that technology adoption proceeded according to the entrepreneurial model. It was therefore to be expected that the executives would not be governed by administrative-type motivations for the adoption of new technologies and would not follow the technology adoption management model – all the more so as we were looking at medium-sized businesses, where we can expect to find entrepreneurial behaviour.

All these proposed explanations, and particularly the as-yet untested constructed dimensions in Stevenson's model, had to be checked against the evidence.

 Check the proposed explanations against the data

The development of explanatory schemes in the data interpretation stage yields explanations through a back-and-forth movement between generating ideas and checking them against the data. In this process, a series of cases is treated as a set of experiments in which each case serves to confirm or disconfirm the researcher's proposed interpretations (Eisenhardt 1989; Yin 2003). The process of testing the explanations against the evidence should therefore be performed using embedded units of analysis, i.e., for a single case at a time. The evidence for all the cases should never be assembled and considered as one unit.

The purpose here is to determine to what extent the data on a case supports the researcher's proposed explanations. In addition to a thorough and focused review of the evidence, asking informants

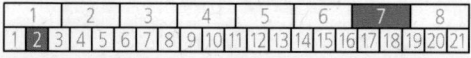

to comment on the possible explanations the researcher has arrived at by studying their case can be a highly effective strategy at this stage (Yin 2003).

A proposition that is not supported by the evidence must be rejected. A proposition that is not fully supported should be revised accordingly. An explanatory scheme that fits one case can then be tested against another case, and so forth. Examining cross-case differences can be highly revealing. Useful methods for testing proposed explanations include establishing differences and similarities, probing the meaning of atypical cases, and examining extreme cases. We should also consider whether opposed interpretations and alternative explanations might also be supported by the evidence, and look for counter-evidence (Stake 1994; Yin 2003).

At what point should the investigator end the back-and-forth movement between generating explanations and testing them against the evidence? This can be done when theoretical saturation appears to have been reached, i.e., when the new proposed explanations are adding little or nothing of theoretical value (Eisenhardt 1989). We must also make sure that the process of iteration and review not make us lose sight of the original aim of the study. To avoid being sidetracked, we should always bear the research question in mind (Yin 2003).

As has been seen, theory building is no simple mechanical task: it is a creative endeavour. Checking the theory against the facts is an integral part of the process, not a subsequent stage (Richards and Richards 1994).

In my study of medium-sized business executives, I began the process of checking my explanations against the evidence by considering whether I had measures for each construct of the dimensions in Stevenson's entrepreneurial/administrative behaviour model. If the results were positive for one case, I proceeded to the next until I had covered the 11 cases in my sample. This test supported my first hypothesis that Stevenson's model fits the behaviour of medium-sized manufacturers, and my second hypothesis to the effect that this model could be applied to specific activities of business executives – to wit, the adoption of new technologies in the cases under examination.

I then tested my central hypothesis, that medium-sized business executives behave as entrepreneurs in the technology adoption process, against my data. For each case, I performed a fit analysis for all five dimensions of Stevenson's model. I then located each case on the overall entrepreneurial/administrative behaviour continuum.

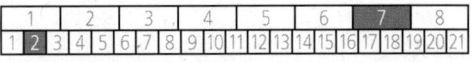

As Chart 4 below shows, while they did not all fall at the far end of the scale, 10 of the 11 medium-sized business executives were on the entrepreneurial side of the chart and the other was very close to the administrative end of the scale. Therefore, the evidence only partially supported my hypothesis; I had to adjust it and conclude that in medium-sized businesses migration to a new technology is an entrepreneurial act in the vast majority of cases but it is entirely possible to find administrative behaviour as well.

Chart 4
Positions of All Cases in Terms of Stevenson's Model

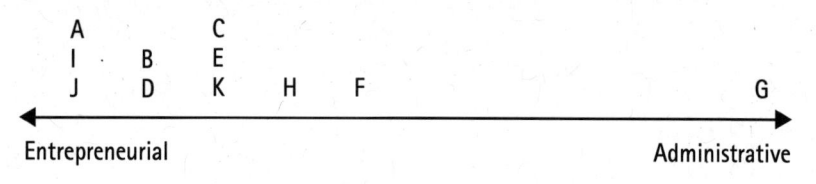

A		C				
I	B	E				
J	D	K	H	F		G

Entrepreneurial   Administrative

STEP 7.3 Compare the proposed explanations that pass the evidence test with the existing literature

When a proposed explanation passes the reality test and is found to fit the evidence, it should then be compared with what is found in the literature. The purpose here is to make a contribution to theory by identifying and analyzing any differences between the proposed explanation and existing theory.

It is very important, at the outset, to compare the concepts, constructs and theoretical propositions we are testing with those that already exist in the literature on the phenomenon of interest. If we find some support in the literature, this buttresses the internal validity of the study and makes it possible to generalize the results. The literature review should include not only studies that are consistent with the proposed explanations that emerge from our research but – just as importantly, if not more so – texts that contradict our own interpretations (Eisenhardt 1989).

One must also make sure there are no alternative explanations for the phenomenon. If any can be found, they too must be tested against the data and, if they pass the test, they should be used to enhance the proposed theoretical framework (Eisenhardt 1989; Stake 1994).

In my study of medium-sized business executives, I found no literature reporting findings or even musings about executive behaviour in the technology adoption process. Our results therefore made a contribution to the existing body of knowledge, but they were hardly generalizable.

I should point out that Stevenson's model was described in the literature but there was no indication that it had been tested. My research therefore made a contribution to validating the model.

However, the data interpretation process will serve little purpose if the results are not disseminated to the scientific and professional community. This is the goal of the final stage.

STAGE 8

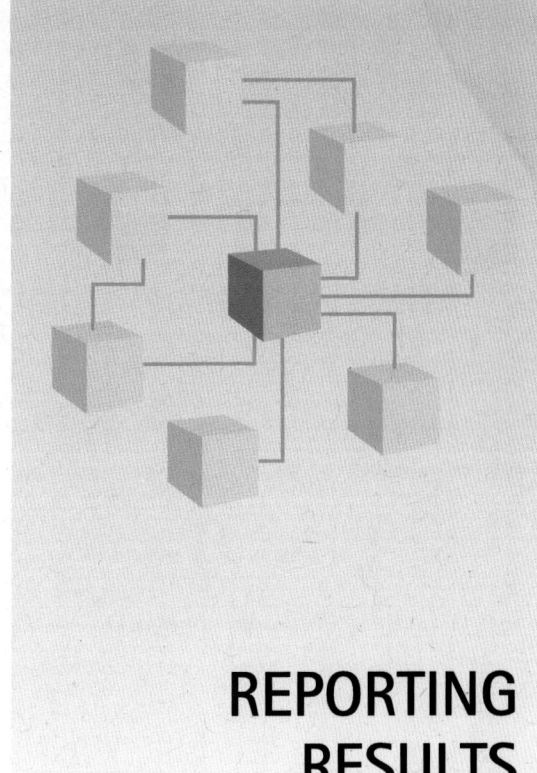

REPORTING
RESULTS

issemination of the results is the ultimate goal of any study. Unless the researcher is narcissistic in the extreme, it makes little sense to devote months and in many cases years to a study if the results will never be published. And it is just as disappointing to publish findings that no one reads or cares about, in which case the research will have no impact on anyone other than the researcher (Richardson 1994).

Carrying out the case study and reporting the findings are two separate stages in the research process that require different skills: analytic and critical thinking to conduct the study, command of style and rhetoric to disseminate the results in a way that is likely to persuade others of their significance and value (Wacheux 2002).

Our purpose here is not to provide a writing guide. There are already a good number of fairly detailed and precise guides available. I will confine myself to noting a few points that should be taken into account when reporting the results of a case study.

STEP 8.1   Decide on the type of report

There are various vehicles for disseminating research results: research reports, articles in academic or professional journals, papers delivered at conferences, which may or may not be published in the conference proceedings, and speeches at other types of events.

The research report is a necessary part of the process. One should be produced for every study, as soon as possible after the data interpretation stage.

The research report is a good way to compile and document all of the study's findings. It should also include a full description of the methodology and the means used to ensure the accuracy of the results. Along with other materials of varying types and significance, such as interview tapes, progress reports and logs, the research report helps explain the analytic and interpretative procedures used by the researcher (Hlady Rispal 2002a, b).

A research report can be used to provide peers with full and detailed information on the history of each case when seeking comments. As well, it can be a practical way to determine the most appropriate vehicle for disseminating the results, given their nature and scope. Writing the research report is also an opportunity to debrief everyone involved in the project, especially when it was carried out by a research team.

The main criteria that may be taken into account in choosing the dissemination vehicle are, first of all, the nature and scope of the findings. For example, if the study proposes a new theory, it should be disseminated to a scientific audience; the researcher might choose to deliver a paper in order to obtain feedback from conference participants. If the results are of a more practical nature, they should be disseminated mainly to professionals through addresses or papers at conferences attended by practitioners. If the findings are significant, dissemination through several vehicles may be warranted; the researcher may wish to report only part of the results in each publication or paper in order to deliver a clearer and more focused message in each.

The researcher's objectives in terms of desired feedback and target number of publications and papers should also be considered. If peer comments are desired, a scientific journal or event would be an appropriate vehicle. The field in which the peer feedback is desired must be determined. The number of publications and papers generated by a study is often important to a researcher, if only because it can affect funding for future research. Publications also contribute to achieving the basic goal of this stage, which is to share the benefits of the study's contribution to knowledge with as many members of the scientific and professional communities as possible. The researcher should therefore use the results skilfully and judiciously to generate as many publications and papers as possible, without of course repeating himself or herself. For example, when possible it can be a good idea to deliver a paper and then rework it, taking into account the comments made by peers, in order to submit it as an article to a scientific or professional journal. This is where working as part of a team can be advantageous, as each investigator can mine the results from a different point of view and disseminate them in his or her field. Particularly in the case of qualitative research, such as a case study, the findings may be of interest to many audiences, not only people working in the lead researcher's field (Richardson 1994).

Finally, it is important to take the characteristics of the dissemination vehicle into account. Clearly, scientific and professional journals and events are not all of the same calibre and have specific target audiences. For example, some take more interest in quantitative research and others in qualitative research. Some have a theoretical bent while others focus on making a practical contribution, based on the target audience and the publisher's priorities. The fields covered by the publication should also be taken into account; it will probably be more difficult to have findings that relate primarily to psychological theory published in a management journal.

 Determine the requirements of the vehicle and characteristics of the target audience

Once we have decided where to report the results, we need to look at the standards and requirements of the chosen vehicle in greater detail (e.g., number of pages in the case of a publication, allotted time in the case of a paper, content and formatting guidelines). Are they looking for a particular theme? We also need to know how the acceptance process works. For example, is it necessary to submit an abstract or summary in order to be considered? It is a good idea to ask the editors or organizers for guidance, and also to find and analyze a few articles or papers they have accepted in the past.

More importantly still, we need to know the characteristics of the vehicle's audience. Does it consist of academics, practitioners or both? In what field or discipline do they work? In the case of papers or lectures in particular, in what venue will it be held and how large is the expected audience? Is the audience local, national or international?

It is very important to have this information before preparing the outline of the article or paper and writing it, for the questions that were used to organize the research will not necessarily be the ones used to structure the article or paper. As noted above, the observation phase of the study is quite distinct from the presentation of the findings. When reporting the results, the focus should be on the questions

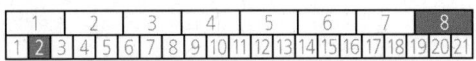

of interest to the audience. This is why many researchers deliberately choose to cater to the audience, even when they know perfectly well that the audience does not share their own concerns with respect to the phenomenon under investigation (Stake 1994).

STEP 8.3 Prepare an outline

An outline helps the researcher report the findings clearly and consistently, and makes for more effective communication with the audience (Létourneau 1989). The audience, as much as the researcher, needs a conceptual structure, a framework, to guide it through the argument (Stake 1994).

Preparing an outline forces us to articulate our thinking, for which we need to possess a good grasp of the study and have assimilated the findings. In the process, the researcher develops a strategy and organizes the available materials to serve a specific purpose, namely to communicate the findings and demonstrate their merit. The demonstration is an ordered argument that strings the information and explanations together into a logical, reasoned sequence (Létourneau 1989).

Before beginning to prepare the outline, the investigator already has a number of ideas, arguments, pieces of information and examples in mind. This is the raw material that must be hammered into shape. The researcher assembles the ideas, groups them together in a logical way, and makes them fit together. The facts and arguments are marshalled to answer the question that is being addressed. The researcher demonstrates the validity of the answer by trying to inform and persuade the audience, arouse their interest and win them over. Just as the research question and strategy have guided the investigator's approach throughout the process, they should now inform the choice of section titles and subtitles, and the main ideas that will be developed in each section (Létourneau 1989).

Richardson (1994) suggests a useful exercise when preparing an outline. She recommends that the researcher begin by choosing an article that typifies the writing conventions used in the mainstream of the discipline and write a two-to-four page analysis of its writing strategies. Then the researcher should do the same thing with an article that he or she feels exemplifies standards of excellence in qualitative research. Finally, the researcher should take a text he or

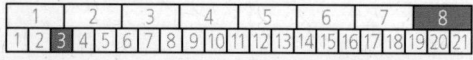

she is proud of having written and consider how it could be improved in light of the analysis of the other two articles. This can be a very valuable exercise that can help establish a solid foundation for the outline of an article or paper on a case study.

8.4 Write the article or paper

Once the outline has been prepared, the researcher is ready to set about writing the article or paper. The main goals here are clarity, conciseness and use of appropriate language (Létourneau 1989). It is very important to include all the information the reader needs in order to assess the validity of the results. Any report, article or paper should provide enough evidence to enable the audience to draw its own conclusions about the case study. An outside observer should be able to trace the evidence-building process from the research question to the conclusions and distinguish the various steps along the way (Yin 2003). It is unfortunate that it is still the exception rather than the rule for an article on a case study to include a discussion of the reliability and validity of the results, a shortcoming that helps maintain prejudices about the rigour of qualitative research methods (Kvale 1987).

This can be quite a challenge when one has to report the results of a study in a 30-minute presentation or a 20-page article. How is it possible to do justice to the complexity of the context, the phenomenon itself and the investigator's intuitions about a particular case within those limits, especially when a number of cases have been studied (Dyer and Wilkins 1991)? Clearly, it is not feasible to report everything that was observed. The researcher must decide what is necessary to a proper understanding of the case and provide enough material so readers can make their own way through the findings (Stake 1994). Elegant writing should be combined with a credible description of the events and interpretations.

We should strive for a discussion that flows and be prepared to drop ideas, arguments, facts and examples that digress. Keeping the content consistent and coherent is one of the central goals when writing a scientific article or paper. All the components should fit together into a logical and cumulative whole (Létourneau 1989). It has been said that the quality of an article or paper depends on the richness of the argument, the credibility of the supporting evidence, and the acuity of the analysis. But other factors are also important, such as the clarity of the discussion, the logical progression of the reasoning,

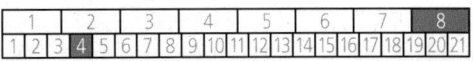

the writing style and the ability to hold the reader's interest. And of course the content must be convincing by virtue of the strength of the arguments and the power of the evidence and facts. Ultimately, the article or paper must be refined and professional if it is to persuade the audience (Létourneau 1989).

The structure of the article or paper should be orderly and methodical. It should follow the outline prepared in the previous step. When introducing a new idea, it is usually advisable to open a new paragraph, section or chapter, and then provide complementary material to explain, support and reinforce the core idea (Létourneau 1989). The sentences are organized, highlighted, subordinated, linked to charts, and strung together with verve and an element of doubt to convey not only the thoughts of participants in the phenomenon of interest but also those of the researcher (Stake 1994).

Without going into detail, this structure should include the basic elements of the study: the problem, the research question, the theoretical framework, the variables, the hypotheses, etc. In ethnographic research, it is also important to mention the investigator's initial assumptions in all articles and papers on the study (Altheide and Johnson 1994). A detailed description of the methodology should then be provided, including the data collection, analysis and interpretation tools and methods (Hlady Rispal 2002a, b), followed by a description of the actions taken in order to guarantee the accuracy of the results. The results *per se* should then be presented, along with all the information readers need to understand the analysis and interpretation of the data by the researcher. Lastly, the conclusion should highlight the study's main contributions to knowledge. It can also be used to draw attention to aspects of the study the researcher considers important, such as the originality of the experimental design or the strength of the analytic method, and to discuss the limitations of the study and suggest avenues for future research (Provost 1997).

Style should not be neglected, for even if the subject is fascinating and the study was very well executed, the article or paper may appear dense and forbidding to the audience. It is therefore advisable to try for some flair and avoid pedantry in reflecting the attention to significant detail that is the essence of qualitative research. The idea is not to put up a façade of objectivity but rather to inscribe the conditions under which the statements were produced in order to enable the reader to assess the reliability and validity of the proposed explanations (Wacheux 2002).

In this sense, stories can be more interesting and compelling than statistical analysis. Not only are they more likely to stick in the mind, but they reflect complexity better than do detailed neutral descriptions, statistical tables or scatter charts (Dyer and Wilkins 1991; Martin and Power 1983). A lively descriptive style and vibrant language make the investigator's experience more vivid and real for readers. As Richardson (1994: 519) puts it, "metaphor is the backbone of social science writing. Like the spine, it bears weight, permits movement, is buried beneath the surface, and links parts together into a functional, coherent whole." Tropes provide a link between the reader's imaginary worlds and the external reality described in the text, and they give shape to the theory-building endeavour (Boothman 2003).

The goal is to write a story that covers the setting, the participants' points of view, and the observer's deductions. It is not unusual for a qualitative researcher to allow a case to tell its own story. Any report on the findings of a case study should include quotes or extracts from evidence provided by informants or other sources (Carter 1993; Coles 1989; Stake 1994). Co-authoring can also be a good way to produce rich stories that reveal all the dimensions of the subject.

As the aim is to hold the attention of the reader or audience, it is preferable to strive for an engaging style when reporting the facts and to turn the interview reports into narratives, using a certain literary flair if possible. The text will then tell a story instead of just listing the facts uncovered by the study (Richardson 1994). One good way to check whether the text is clear and compelling is to show it to a layperson and find out whether he or she finds the subject interesting and the conclusions understandable.

As the researcher works on the article or paper, it may be useful to do further reading in order to refine an argument, add an example or clarify a point. It is never too late to enrich the argument with new material, provided it does not digress from the main thrust (Létourneau 1989).

With the dissemination of the results, all the stages in the process of using the case study as a research method have been completed.

CONCLUSION

By way of conclusion, I hope I can say, "mission accomplished." My objective in writing this handbook was two-pronged: to equip researchers to make an informed decision on whether the case method is appropriate to their research, and if so, to provide them with a step-by-step guide to conducting a case study with scientific rigour. The first chapter, which discusses how to determine the appropriateness of the case method, is intended to address the first part of this objective. The following chapters, which describe in detail the stages and steps that should be carried out to ensure accurate results (preparation, case selection, data collection, analysis and interpretation, and finally reporting the findings) are intended to address the second part. It is my hope that they will serve researchers as a comprehensive practical guide to conducting a case study.

Reading or, better yet, using this guide should demonstrate that the case study is indeed a scientific research method. The orderly sequence of stages illustrates the logical, scientific procedure the case researcher must follow. The steps in this handbook describe the specific activities that should be carried out in order to produce evidence and theory that are clear, logical and irrefutable, in keeping with the scientific method. In particular, the emphasis placed on principles of data collection, analysis and, above all, interpretation, and the description of the many steps designed to ensure accurate results, should serve to support a scientifically rigorous approach.

The case method is fruitful in that it makes it possible to study a phenomenon not only in itself but also in its natural setting, whether it be to build or to test a theory. The case study permits systematic investigation of the phenomenon by examining the dynamic interrelationships among managerial/regulatory processes, social interactions and collective outputs related to the phenomenon of interest. It is then possible to develop an analogical, non-linear narrative that embraces the causal relationships in the systems under study (Beaucourt and Louart 2002; Bergadaa 2002).

However, conducting a case study for research purposes is both demanding and complex, as this handbook shows, even as it demonstrates the usefulness and – dare I say it? – necessity of the case method. It provides a step-by-step guide to a process that is both delicate and complicated, one that involves a multitude of details, none of which can be neglected. As Eisenhardt (1989) stresses, the quality of a case study largely depends on the rigour with which the researcher approaches each stage of the research process. And what is still more, the stages and steps must be conducted iteratively, not sequentially.

More generally, using the case method for research purposes poses three main challenges, which this handbook describes and attempts to equip researchers to address. The first is the challenge of field management: the investigator must use interpersonal skills to win acceptance, obtain the required information, control for the effects of his or her presence, and share his or her analyses with the informants. There is also an ethical dimension here, since the researcher is intervening directly in a human setting when collecting confidential information from numerous informants. Standard ethical rules must be scrupulously observed. Moreover, the investigator must behave in such a way that the subjects will have no qualms about taking part in another study and indeed will be happy to do it, in light of their experience. It is also important to treat confidential information as such at all times and to protect the anonymity of the sources, unless the informants have specifically agreed to be identified.

The second challenge, tool management, is of a more technical nature: the researcher must make the right decisions in formalizing the research framework and choosing and/or developing data collection, analysis and interpretation instruments.

The third and last challenge, data management, is both strategic and scientific. It involves producing results that are accurate and useful. The researcher can meet this challenge by taking measures to ensure the reliability and validity of the collected evidence (Hlady Rispal 2002).

To conclude, I can only repeat my hope this handbook has shown the usefulness of the case method as one tool in the researcher's methodological arsenal and that it will serve the reader in good stead.

APPENDIX

STEP-BY-STEP CHECKLIST

STAGE 1 – ASSESSING APPROPRIATENESS

STEP   DONE

1. Have you defined your approach?   ☐

2. Have you outlined the research problem?   ☐

3. Is the problem of the exploratory or raw empirical type?   ☐

4. Have you answered preset questions to determine the   ☐
    appropriateness of conducting a case study?

STAGE 2 – ENSURING ACCURACY

Internal reliability

STEP   DONE

1. Are you using concrete and precise descriptors?   ☐

2. Is the raw data available?   ☐

3. Have you been able to involve several researchers on the project?   ☐

4. Has the collected data been confirmed by the informants?   ☐

5. Has the interpretation of the data been reviewed by peers?   ☐

External reliability

STEP   DONE

6. Have you established your own position?   ☐

7. Can you describe the informant selection process and demonstrate   ☐
    its soundness?

8. Have the relevant physical, social and interpersonal characteristics ☐
    of each research setting been described?

9. Have you clearly defined the study's concepts, constructs and units ☐
    of analysis?

10. Can you describe the data collection strategy in detail?   ☐

Internal validity

STEP   DONE

11. Have you controlled for the effects of the observer's presence?   ☐

12. Have you selected a representative sample?   ☐

13. Have you developed and maintained a chain of meaning and a data   ☐
    definition table for each case?

14. Have you identified and excluded alternative explanations?   ☐

External validity

STEP		DONE
15.	Have you controlled for the effects of study site specificities?	☐
16.	Have you avoided over-studied sites?	☐
17.	Have you chosen cases that are replicable over time and maintained an up-to-date history of each?	☐

Construct validity

STEP		DONE
18.	Have you selected cases with characteristics that meet the initial research objectives?	☐
19.	Are the measures you are using for purposes of data collection, analysis and interpretation appropriate?	☐
20.	Have you used as many information sources as possible and used triangulation?	☐
21.	Can you explain the research protocol and present the data honestly?	☐

STAGE 3 – PREPARATION

STEP		DONE
1.	Have you framed the research question?	☐
2.	Have you decided on a single- or multiple-case study?	☐
3.	Have you determined the main data collection technique and potential data sources?	☐
4.	Have you established the case selection criteria?	☐
5.	Have data coding instruments and protocols, and a data coding scheme, been developed?	☐
6.	Have you familiarized yourself with the phenomenon of interest?	☐

STAGE 4 – SELECTING CASES

STEP		DONE
1.	Have you acquired a thorough knowledge of the workings of the environment under study?	☐
2.	Have you checked that you have no other professional relationship with the subjects?	☐
3.	Is the geographic distribution of cases practical?	☐
4.	Have you recruited at least one more than the necessary number of cases to ensure rigour?	☐

STAGE 5 – COLLECTING DATA

STEP   DONE

1. Have you gained acceptance in the research setting?   ☐

2. Have you used your observation and active listening skills?   ☐

3. Have you used as many information sources as possible?   ☐

4. Have you fine-tuned the data collection strategy and adapted it to   ☐
   each case?

5. Have you maintained an updated data definition table and a chain   ☐
   of meaning for the collected data?

6. Has the collected data been managed in a structured and orderly   ☐
   manner?

7. Have you made a smooth exit from the research sites?   ☐

STAGE 6 – ANALYZING DATA

STEP   DONE

1. Has the collected data been purged?   ☐

2. Have you coded the collected data on each case?   ☐

3. Has the coded data been analyzed?   ☐

4. Have you written a description of each case?   ☐

STAGE 7 – INTERPRETING DATA

STEP   DONE

1. Have you generated proposed explanations of the phenomenon   ☐
   based on the results of the data analysis?

2. Have the proposed explanations been checked against the data?   ☐

3. Have the proposed explanations that pass the evidence test been   ☐
   compared with the existing literature?

STAGE 8 – REPORTING RESULTS

STEP   DONE

1. Have you decided on the type of report?   ☐

2. Have the requirements of the vehicle and characteristics of the   ☐
   target audience been determined?

3. Have you prepared an outline?   ☐

4. Have you written the article or paper?   ☐

REFERENCES

Agar, M. (1991). "The Right Brain Strikes Back," in N.G. Fielding and R.M. Lee (ed.), *Using Computers in Qualitative Research*, London: Sage, 181–193.

Agger, B. (1990). *The Decline of Discourse: Reading, Writing and Resistance in Post-modern Capitalism*, Bristol, PA: Falmer.

Aktouf, O. (1987). *Méthodologie des sciences sociales et approche qualitative des organisations*, Sillery: Presses de l'Université du Québec.

Allison, G. and P. Zelikow (1999). *Essence of Decision: Explaining the Cuban Missile Crisis*, New York: Addison-Wesley.

Altheide, D.L. and J.M. Johnson (1994). " Criteria for Assessing Interpretive Validity in Qualitative Research," N.K. Denzin and Y.S. Lincoln (dir.), *Handbook of Qualitative Research*, Thousand Oaks: Sage, 485–499.

Anderson, P. (1983). "Decision Making by Objection and the Cuban Missile Crisis," *Administrative Science Quarterly 28*: 201–222.

Andrew, W. (1985). "The Phenomenological Foundations for Empirical Methodology II: The Method of Optional Variations," *Journal of Phenomenological Psychology 16*: 1–29.

Bachelor, A. (1992). "On the Use of Judges in Phenomenological Empirical Research," *Methods*, 1–25.

Bachelor, A. and P. Joshi (1986). *La méthode phénoménologique de la recherche en psychologie*, Québec: Presses de l'Université Laval.

Bagchi, D.K., P. Blaikie, J. Cameron, M. Chattopadhyay, N. Gyawali and D. Seddon (1998). "Conceptual and Methodological Challenges in the Study of Livelihood Trajectories: Case-Studies in Eastern India and Western Nepal," *Journal of International Development 10*: 453–468.

Bardin, L. (1996). *L'analyse de contenu* (8th ed.), Paris: Presses universitaires de France.

Beaucourt, C. and P. Louart (2002). "Pour un libre usage de la méthode des cas en Sciences de gestion," in *Journée d'étude "La méthode des cas,"* Pessac, France: Université Montesquieu-Bordeaux IV.

Becker, H.S. (1958). "Problem of Inference and Proof in Participant Observation," *American Sociological Review 23*: 652–660.

Becker, H., B. Geer, A. Strauss and E.C. Hughes (1961). *Boys in White*, New Brunswick, NJ: Transaction Books.

Benbasat, I. (1984). "An Analysis of Research Methodologies," in F. Warren McFarlan (ed.), *The Information Systems Research Challenge*, Boston: Harvard Business School Press, 47–85.

Benbasat, I., D.K. Goldstein and M. Mead (1983). "The Case Research Strategy in Studies of Information Systems," *MIS Quarterly 11*(3): 369–386.

Berelson, B. (1952). *Content Analysis in Communication Research*, Glencoe, IL: Free Press.

Bergadaa, M. (2002). "Expérience pédagogique de réalisation de cas en gestion avec des étudiants de 3e cycle," in *Journée d'étude "La méthode des cas,"* Pessac, France: Université Montesquieu-Bordeaux IV.

Berk, R. (1979). "Generalizability of Behavioral Observations: A Clarification of Inter-observer Agreement and Interobserver Reliability," *American Journal of Mental Deficiency 83*: 460–472.

Beutler, L. and D. Hamblin (1986). "Individualized Outcome Measures of Internal Change: Methodological Considerations," *Journal of Consulting and Clinical Psychology 54*: 48–53.

Blau, P.M. (1955). *The Dynamics of Bureaucracy*, Chicago: University of Chicago Press.

Bogdan, R.C. and S.J. Taylor (1975). *Introduction to Qualitative Research Methods: A Phenomenological Approach to the Social Sciences*, New York: Wiley.

Boje, D. (1991). "The Story Telling Organization: A Study of Story Performance in an Office Supply Firm," *Administrative Science Quarterly 36*: 106–126.

Bonoma, T.V. (1983). *A Case Study in Case Research: Marketing Implementation*, Working Paper 9-585-142, Boston: Harvard University Graduate School of Business Administration.

Boothman, N. (2003). *Tout se joue en moins de 2 minutes: La première impression que l'on donne est celle qui reste...*, Paris: Marabout.

Bullock, R. (1986). "A Meta-Analysis Method for OD Case Studies," *Group and Organization Studies 11*(1–2): 33–48.

Bryman, A. and R.G. Burgess (1994). "Reflections on Qualitative Data Analysis," in A. Ryman and R.G. Burgess (ed.), *Analysing Qualitative Data*, London: Routledge, 216–226.

Canada Council (1977). *Ethics*, Report of the Consultative Group on Ethics.

Carmines, F. and R. Zeller (1979). *Reliability and Validity Assessment*, Thousand Oaks: Sage.

Carter, K. (1993). "The Place of Story in the Study of Teaching and Teacher Education," *Educational Researcher 22*: 5–12.

Catterall, M. and P. Maclaran (1996). "Using Computer Program to Code Qualitative Data," *Marketing Intelligence and Planning 14*(4): 26–33.

Clandinin, D.J. (1994). "Personal Experience Methods," in M.K. Denzin and Y.S. Lincoln (ed.), *Handbook of Qualitative Research*, Thousand Oaks: Sage, 413–427.

Coles, R. (1989). *The Call of Stories: Teaching and the Moral Imagination*, Boston: Houghton Mifflin.

Cone, J.O. and S.L. Foster (1982). "Direct Observation in Clinical Psychology," in P. Kendall and J. Butcher (ed.), *Handbook of Research Methods in Clinical Psychology*, New York: Wiley, 311–353.

Cook, T.D. and D.T. Campbell (1979). *Quasi-experimentation: Design and Analysis Issues for Field Settings*, Chicago: Rand McNally. CRONBACH, L.J. (1975). "Beyond the Two Disciplines of Scientific Psychology," *American Psychologist 30*: 116–127.

Crozier, M. (1964). *The Bureaucratic Phenomenon*, London: Tavistock Publications.

Dabbs, J.M. Jr. (1982). "Making Things Visible," in J. Van Maanen, James M. Dabbs and Robert R. Faulkner (ed.), *Varieties of Qualitative Research*, Beverly Hills: Sage, 31–63.

Denno, D.W. (2003). "A Mind to Blame: New Views on Involuntary Acts," *Behavioral Sciences and the Law 21*: 601–618.

De Weerd-Nederhof, P.C. (2001). "Qualitative Case Study Research, the Case of a Ph.D. Research Project on Organising and Managing New Development Systems," *Management Decision 39*(7): 513–538.

Dey, I. (1993). *Qualitative Data Analysis: A User Friendly Guide for Social Scientists*, London: Routledge.

Denzin, N.K. (1978). *The Research Act: A Theoretical Introduction to Sociological Methods* (2nd ed.), New York: McGraw-Hill.

Diener, E. and R. Crandall (1977). *Ethics in Social and Behavioral Research*, Chicago: University of Chicago Press.

Drass, K.A. (1980). "The Analysis of Qualitative Data: A Computer Program," *Urban Life 9*: 322–253.

Drass, K.A. (1989). "Test Analysis and Text-Analysis Software: A Comparison of Assumptions," in Blank, G., J.L. McCartney and E. Brent (ed.), *New Terminology in Sociology: Practical Applications in Research and Work*, New Brunswick, NJ: Transaction Publishers.

Dyer, W.G. Jr. and A.L. Wilkins (1991). "Better Stories, not better Constructs, to Generate better Stories: A Rejoinder to Eisenhardt," *Academy of Management Review 16*(3): 613–619.

Eisenhardt, K.M. (1989). "Building Theories from Case Study Research," *Academy of Management Review 14*(4): 532–550.

Eisenhardt, K.M. and L.J. Bourgeois III (1988). "Politics of Strategic Decision Making in High-Velocity Environments: Toward a Midrange Theory," *Academy of Management Journal 31*(4): 737–770.

Elliott, R. (1989). "Comprehensive Process Analysis: Understanding the Change Process in Significant Therapy Events," in M. Packer and R. Addison (ed.), *Entering the Circle: Hermeneutic Investigation in Psychology*, New York: State University of New York Press, 165–184.

Fauconnier, G. (1997). *Mapping in Thought and Language*, Cambridge, UK: Cambridge University Press.

Fernandez, R. (2001). "Skill-biased Technological Change and Wage Inequality: Evidence from a Plant Retooling," *The American Journal of Sociology 107*(2): 273–320.

Fielding, N.G. (1993). "Qualitative Data Analysis with a Computer: Recent Developments," *Social Research Update*, 1, www.soc.surrey.ac.uk/sru/SRU1.html.

Franz, C.R. and D. Robey (1984). "An Investigation of User-Led System Design: Rational and Political Perspectives," *Communication of the ACM 27*(12): 1202–1217.

Gagnon, Y.-C. (2001). "The Behavior of Public Managers in Adopting New Technologies," *Public Performance and Management Review 24*(4): 337–350.

Gagnon, Y.-C. and M. Landry (1989). "Les changements technologiques: une stratégie d'étude exploratoire," *Relations industrielles 44*(2): 421–446.

Gagnon, Y.-C., H. Sicotte and E. Posada (2000). "Impact of SME Manager's Behavior on the Adoption of Technology," *Entrepreneurship, Theory and Practice 25*(2): 43–57.

Gagnon, Y.-C. and J.-M. Toulouse (1993). "Adopting News Technologies: An Entrepreneurial Act," *Technovation 13*(7): 411–424.

Gagnon, Y.-C. and J.-M. Toulouse (1996). "The Behavior of Business Managers when Adopting New Technologies," *Technological Forecasting and Social Change 52*(1): 59–74.

Gersick, C. (1988). "Time and Transition in Work Learns: Toward a New Model of Group Development," *Academy of Management Journal 31*: 9–41.

Gladwin, C.H. (1989). *Ethnographic Decision Tree Modeling*, Thousand Oaks: Sage.

Glaser, B.G. and A. Strauss (1967). *The Discovery of Grounded Theory*, Chicago: Aldine.

Goffman, E. (1959). *The Presentation of Self in Everyday Life*, Garden City, NY: Doubleday.

Guba, Egon G. (1981). "Criteria for Assessing the Trustworthiness of Naturalistic Inquiries," *Educational Communication and Technology Journal 29*(2): 75–91.

Hagedorn, R. (1983). "Current Perspectives in Sociological Research," in R. Hagedorn (ed.), *Sociology* (2nd ed.), Toronto: Holt Rinehart, 11–19.

Halling, S. and M. Leifer (1991). "The Theory and Practice of Dialogal Research," *Journal of Phenomenological Psychology 22*: 1–15.

Harris, S. and R. Sutton (1986). "Functions of Parting Ceremonies in Dying Organizations," *Academy of Management Journal 29*: 5–30.

Heise, D. (1992). *Ethnograph* (2nd ed.), Chapel Hill: University of North Carolina Press.

Hersen, M. and D.H. Barlow (1976). *Single-Case Experimental Design: Strategies for Studying Behavior Change*, New York: Pergamon.

Hill, C., K. O'Grady and P. Price (1988). "A Method for Investigating Sources of Rater Bias," *Journal of Counselling Psychology 35*: 346–350.

Hlady Rispal, M. (2002a). "Méthode de l'étude de cas: Les défis du chercheur en gestion," in *Journée d'étude "La méthode des cas,"* Pessac, France: Université Montesquieu-Bordeaux IV.

Hlady Rispal, M. (2002b). "La méthode des cas: Application à la recherche en gestion," in *Journée d'étude "La méthode des cas,"* Pessac, France: Université Montesquieu-Bordeaux IV.

Howard, J.A. and W.M. Morgenroth (1968). "Information Processing Model of Executive Decision," *Management Science 14*: 416–428.

Huberman, A.M. and M.B. Miles (1991). *Analyse des données qualitatives, recueil de nouvelles méthodes*, Brussels: De Boeck.

Jick, T.D. (1979). "Mixing Qualitative and Quantitative Methods: Triangulation in Action," *Administrative Science Quarterly 24*: 602–611.

Kennedy, M.M. (1979). "Generalizing from Single Case Studies," *Evaluation Quarterly 3*: 661–678.

Kidder, T. (1982). *Soul of a New Machine*, New York: Avon.

Kracauer, S. (1993). "The Challenge to Qualitative Content Analysis," *Public Opinion Quarterly 16*: 631–642.

Kvale, S. (1987). "Validity in the Qualitative Research Interview," *Methods 2*: 1–37.

Landry, F. and J. Farr (1980). "Performance Rating," *Psychological Bulletin 87*: 72–107.

Landry, M., J.-L. Malouin and M. Oral (1985). "La validation des modèles en recherche opérationnelle," *AFCET/Interfaces 31*: 919.

Lecompte, M.D. and J.P. Goetz (1982). "Problems of Reliability and Validity in Ethno-graphic," *Review of Educational Research 52*(1): 31–60.

Lécuyer, R. (1987). "L'analyse de contenu: notion et étapes," in J.-P. Deslauriers (ed.), *Les méthodes de la recherche qualitative*, Sillery: Presses de l'Université du Québec, 49–65.

Lehman, D. (1991). *Signs of the Times: Deconstruction and the Fall of Paul de Man*, New York: Poseidon.

Létourneau, J. (1989). *Le coffre à outils du chercheur débutant, guide d'initiation au travail intellectuel*, Toronto: Oxford University Press.

Light, D. Jr. (1979). "Surface Data and Deep Structure: Observing the Organization of Professional Training," *Administrative Science Quarterly 24*(4): 551–559.

Light, R.J., J.D. Singer and J.B. Willett (1990). *By Design: Planning Research on Higher Education*, Cambridge, MA: Harvard University Press.

Lipset, S.M., M.A. Trow and J.S. Coleman (1956). *Union Democracy*, New York: Free Press.

Lyotard, J.-F. (1979). *La condition postmoderne: rapport sur le savoir*, Paris: Éditions de Minuit.

Lucas, W.A. (1974). *The Case Survey Method: Aggregating Case Experience*, document number 1515-Rc, Santa Monica: Rand Corporation.

McMillan, J. and S. Schumacher (1984). "Ethnographic Research," in J. McMillan and S. Schumacher (ed.), *Research in Education: A Conceptual Introduction*, Boston: Little Brown, 305–333.

Manning, P.K. and B. Cullum-Swan (1994). "Narrative, Content and Semiotic Analysis," in N.K. Denzin and Y.S. Lincoln (ed.), *Handbook of Qualitative Research* (1st ed.), Thousand Oaks: Sage, 463–473.

Martin, J. and M. Powers (1983). "Truth or Corporate Propaganda: The Value of a Good War Story" in L. Pondy, P. Frost, G. Morgan and T. C. Dandridge (ed.), *Organizational Symbolism*, Greenwich, CT: JAI Press, 93–107.

Miles, M.B. (1979). "Qualitative Data as an Attractive Nuisance: The Problem of Analysis," *Administrative Science Quarterly 24*(4): 590–602.

Miles, M.B. and A.M. Huberman (1994). *Qualitative Data Analysis: An Expanded Source-book* (2nd ed.), London: Sage.

Mintzberg, H. (1979). "An Emerging Strategy of 'Direct' Research," *Administrative Science Quarterly 24*: 580–589.

Mintzberg, H. and J. Waters (1982). "Tracking Strategy in an Entrepreneurial Firm," *Academy of Management Journal 25*: 465–499.

Murphy, J.T. (1980). *Getting the Facts: A Fieldwork Guide for Evaluators and Policy Analysts*, Santa Monica: Goodyear.

Ogbu, J.U. (1974). *The Next Generation: An Ethnography of Education in an Urban Neighbourhood*, New York: Academic Press.

Patton, M.C. (1980). *Qualitative Evaluation Methods*, London: Sage.

Patton, M.C. (1982). "Qualitative Methods and Approaches: What Are They ?," in E. Kuhns and S. V. Mortorana (ed.), *Qualitative Methods for Institutional Research*, San Francisco: Jossey-Bass, 3–16.

Pinfield, L. (1986). "A Field Evaluation of Perspectives on Organizational Decision Making," *Administrative Science Quarterly 32*: 365–388.

Pinto, G. and M. Grawitz (1969). *Méthodes des sciences sociales*, Paris: Dalloz.

Provost, M.-A., A. Michel, Y. Leroux and Y. Lussier (1997). *Guide de présentation d'un rapport de recherche* (3rd ed.), Trois-Rivières: Les Éditions SMG.

Przeworski, A. and M.G. NEWMAN (2004). "Palmtop Computer-Assisted Group Therapy for Social Phobia," *Journal of Clinical Psychology 60*(2): 179–188.

Richards, T.J. and L. Richards (1991). "The Transformation of Qualitative Method," in N.G. Fielding and R.M. Lee (ed.), *Using Computers in Qualitative Research*, London: Sage, 38–53.

Richards, T.J. and L. Richards (1994). "Case Studies," in N.K. Denzin and Y.S. Lincoln (ed.), *Handbook of Qualitative Research*, Thousand Oaks: Sage.

Richardson, L. (1994). "Writing: A Method of Inquiry," in N.K. Denzin and Y.S. Lincoln (ed.), *Handbook of Qualitative Research*, Thousand Oaks: Sage, 516–529.

Roethlisberger, F.J. (1977). *The Elusive Phenomena: An Autobiographical Account of My Work in the Field of Organizational Behavior at Harvard Business School*, Boston: Harvard University Press.

Romano, C.A. (1988). "Research Strategies for Small Business: A Case Study Approach," *International Small Business Journal 7*(4): 35–43.

Rothe, J.P. (1982). "Researching Native Education: An Ethnomethodological Perspective," *Canadian Journal of Native Education 9*(4): 1–11.

Rubin, H. and I.S. Rubin (1995). *Qualitative Interviewing: the Art of Hearing Data*, Thousand Oaks: Sage.

Schank, R.C. (1998). *Dynamic Memory Revisited*, New York: Cambridge University Press.

Schatzman, L, and A. Strauss (1973). *Field Research*, Englewood Cliffs, NJ: Prentice-Hall.

Scholz, R.W. and O. Tictje (2001). *Embedded Case Study Methods: Integrating Quantitative and Qualitative Knowledge*, Thousand Oaks: Sage.

Schwartz, M.S. and C.G. Schwartz (1955). "Problems in Participant Observation," *American Journal of Sociology 60*: 343–354.

Seidel, J.V. (1991). "Method and Madness in the Application of Computer Technology to Qualitative Data Analysis," in N.G. Fielding and R.M. Lee (ed.), *Using Computers in Qualitative Research*, London: Sage, 181–193.

Seidel, J.V. and J.A. Clark (1982). "Computers and Ethnography: A Review of Recent Developments in the Use of Computers in Ethnographic Research," conference at the American Sociological Association annual meeting.

Seidel, J.V. and J.A. Clark (1984). "A computer program for the analysis of qualitative data," *Qualitative Sociology 7*(1–2): 110–125.

Selznick, P. (1966). *T.V.A. and the Grass Roots*, Berkeley: University of California Press.

Shapiro, W.L., R. Clemente, L.W. Anglin and P.B. Richard (1993). "Metamorph: Computer Support for Qualitative Research," *Mid-Western Education Researcher 6*(2): 30–34.

Sohal, A., A. Simon and E. Lu (1996). "Generative and Case Study Research in Quality Management: Part 2 – Practical Examples," *International Journal of Quality and Reliability Management 13*(2): 75–87.

Stake, R.E. (1994). "Case Studies," in N.K. Denzin and Y.S. Lincoln (ed.), *Handbook of Qualitative Research*, Thousand Oaks: Sage, 236–247.

Stake, R.E. (1995). *The Art of Case Study Research*, London: Sage.

Stevenson, H.H. (1983). "A New Paradigm for Entrepreneurial Management," in J.J. Kao and H.H. Stevenson (ed.), *Entrepreneurship What It Is and How to Teach It*, Boston: Harvard Business Administration, 30–61.

Stevenson, H.H. (1984). *A Perspective on Entrepreneurship,* Working Paper 9-384-131, Boston: Harvard Business School.

Stevenson, H.H. (1986). *Entrepreneurship: A Response to Discontinuous Change*, Boston: Harvard Business School.

Strauss, A. and J. Corbin (1990). *Basics of Qualitative Research: Grounded Theory Procedures and Techniques*, London: Sage.

Sutton, R.I. and A.L. Callaban (1987). "The Stigma of Bankruptcy: Spoiled Organizational Image and its Management," *Academy of Management Journal 30*: 405–436.

Taylor, S.J. and R. Bogdan (1984). *Introduction to Qualitative Research Methods* (2nd ed.), New York: Wiley.

Tesch, R. (1990). *Qualitative Research: Analysis Types and Software Tools*, Lewes East Sussex, The Falmer Press.

Van Maanen, J. (1979). "The Fact of Fiction in Organizational Ethnography," *Administrative Science Quarterly 24*: 539–550.

Van Maanen, J. (1988). *Tales of the Field: On Writing Ethnography*, Chicago: University of Chicago Press.

Van Someren, M.W., Y.F. Barnard and J.A.C. Sandberg (1994). *The Think Aloud Method*, London: Academic Press.

Wacheux, Frédéric (2002). "Rêverie épistémologique autour de l'étude de cas," in *Journée d'étude "La méthode des cas,"* Pessac, France: Université Montesquieu-Bordeaux IV.

Webb, E., D.T. Campbell, R.D. Schwartz and L. Sechrest (1999). *Unobtrusive Measures* (2nd ed.), Thousand Oaks: Sage.

Wegner, D.M. (2002). *The Illusion of Conscious Well*, Cambridge, MA: MIT Press.

Weick, K.E. (1984). "Theorical Assumptions and Research Methodology Selection," in F. Warren McFarlan (ed.), *The Information Systems Research Challenge*, Boston: Harvard Business School Press, 111–132.

Weitzman, E. and M.B. Miles (1995). *Computer Programs for Qualitative Data Analysis*, London: Sage.

Whyte, W.F. (1963). "Street Corner Society: The Social Structure of an Italian Slum," in M.W. Riley (ed.), *Sociological Research*, New York: Harcourt Brace, 44–56 and 62–77.

Witte, E. (1972). "Field Research on Complex Decision-Making Processes – The Phase Theorem," *International Studies of Management and Organization 2*: 156–182.

Woodside, A.G. and E.J. Wilson (2000). "Constructing Thick Descriptions of Marketers' and Buyers' Decision Processes in Business-to-Business Relationships," *Journal of Business and Industrial Marketing 15*(5): 354–369.

Woodside, A.G. and E.J. Wilson (2003). "Case Study Research Methods for Theory Building," *Journal of Business and Industrial Marketing 18*(6/7): 493–508.

Worthman, M.S. and G.B. Roberts (1982). "Innovative Qualitative Methods, Technique and Design in Strategic Management Research," communication at the Strategic Management Society Conference, Montréal.

Yin, R.K. (1981a). "The Case Study as a Serious Research Strategy," *Science Communication 3*(1): 97–114.

Yin, R.K. (1981b). "The Case Study Crisis: Some Answers," *Administrative Science Quarterly 26*(1): 58–65.

Yin, R.K. (2003). *Case Study Research, Design and Methods* (3rd ed.), Thousand Oaks: Sage.

Yin, R.K., P.G. Bateman and G.B. Moore (1983). *Case Studies and Organizational Innovation: Strengthening the Connection*, Washington, DC: Cosmos Corporation.

Zaltman, G. (2003). *How Customers Think*, Boston: Harvard Business School Press.

Marquis Book Printing Inc.

Québec, Canada

2010

 Recycled
Supporting responsible use
of forest resources
www.fsc.org Cert no. SGS-COC-003153
© 1996 Forest Stewardship Council
FSC   100%

        This book has been printed on 100% post consumer
100%   waste paper, certified Eco-logo and processed chlorine free.